The Marsh in May

and 30 Poems with 29 paintings by Ronald Rand

Ronald Rand

Foreword by
Lawrence Knorr, Ph.D.

including artwork by
Jean-Claude Van Itallie, Martha Carpenter, and Maribee

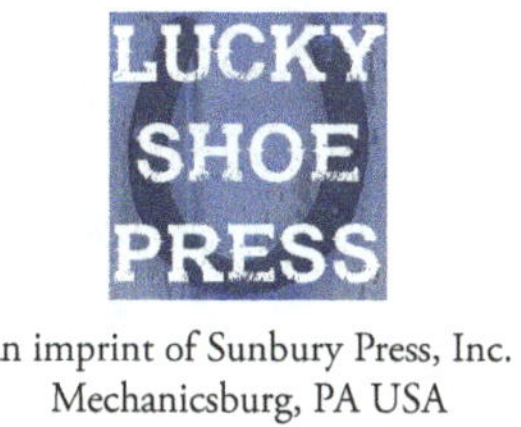

an imprint of Sunbury Press, Inc.
Mechanicsburg, PA USA

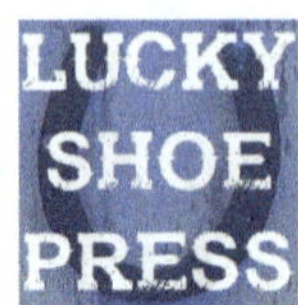

an imprint of Sunbury Press, Inc.
Mechanicsburg, PA USA

FIRST LUCKY SHOE PRESS EDITION: October 2025

Set in Adobe Garamond Pro | Interior design by Crystal Devine | Cover design by Lawrence Knorr. Cover art by Ronald Rand | Edited by Olivia Neri.

Publisher's Cataloging-in-Publication Data
Names: Rand, Ronald, author.
Title: The Marsh in May and 30 poems with 29 paintings by Ronald Rand / Ronald Rand.
Description: First trade paperback edition. | Mechanicsburg, PA : Lucky Shoe Press, 2025.
Summary: *The Marsh in May and 30 Poems with 29 paintings by Ronald Rand* is an unforgettable journey of soaring poetry on nature and the joys and mysteries of life, accompanied by twenty-nine full-color, luminous paintings.
Identifiers: ISBN : 979-8-88819-323-5 (paperback).
Subjects: POETRY / Subjects & Themes / Animals & Nature | POETRY / Subjects & Themes / Motivational & Inspirational | POETRY / Subjects & Themes / Places | ART / Individual Artists / Artists' Books.

Designed in the USA
0 1 1 2 3 5 8 13 21 34 55

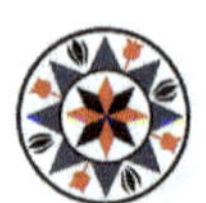

For the Love of Books!

For
Janice Berliner

my dear friends, Rita Fredricks,
Marilise Tronto, and Joyce Maio

and in memory of
Nancy Rhodes

"Nature is the source of all true knowledge."

—Leonardo da Vinci

"When in doubt, tell the truth."

—Mark Twain

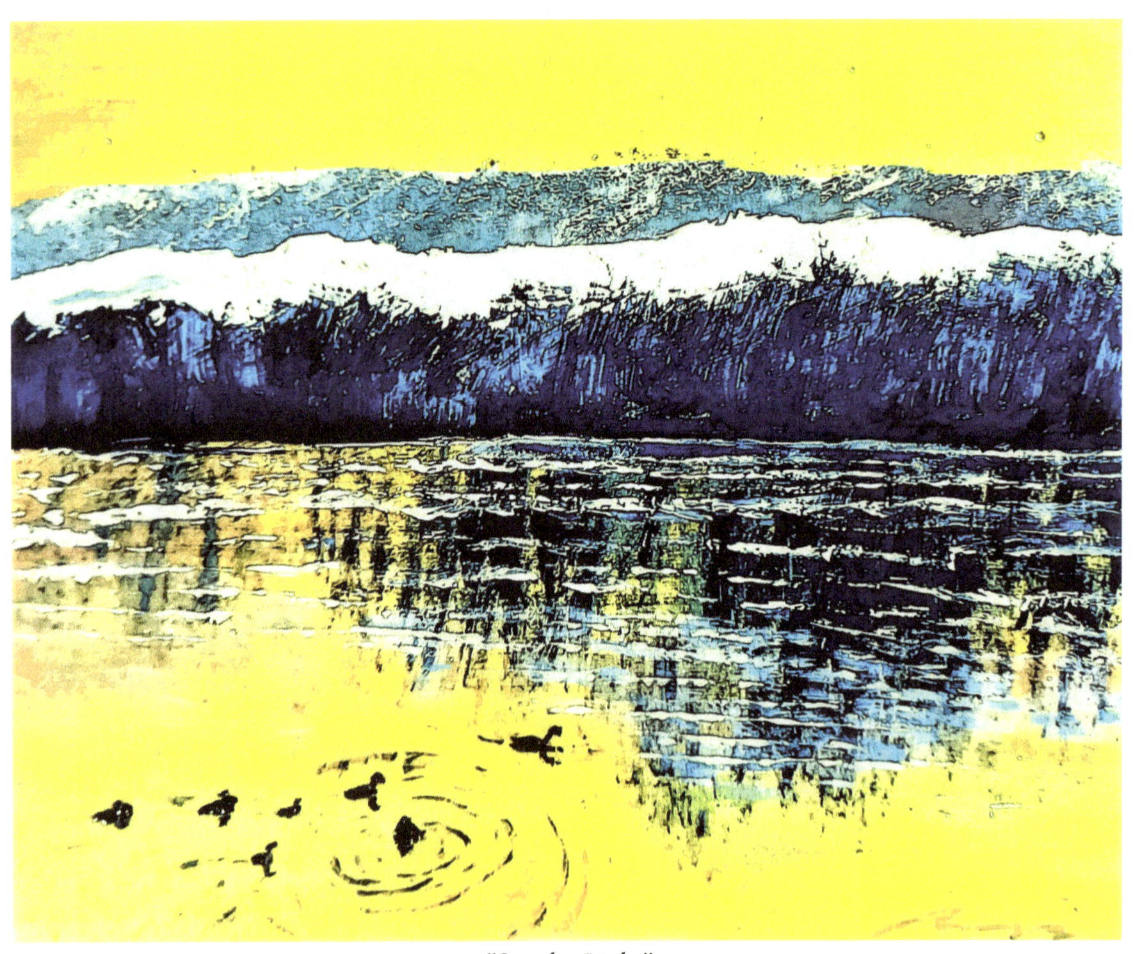

"See the Light"

Contents & Illustrations

All Illustrations by Ronald Rand (artist's name: Ronjay) except where noted

Also by Ronald Rand

Solo Transformation on Stage

CREATE!
How Extraordinary People Live to Create and Create to Live

Acting Teachers of America

Foreword

I first "met" Ronald Rand in 2021 when we published his book about acting, *Solo Transformation on Stage: A Journey into the Organic Process of the Art of Transformation*. At that moment, we at Sunbury Press did not have a sense of Ronald's vast connections and talents. We merely assessed a well-written manuscript from someone passionate about acting on stage. The book's sales were up and down, and Ronald's name popped up infrequently, usually when someone he referred contacted us. First was director Nancy Rhodes, and then actor Laurence Luckinbill. We published books for both.

Then came our visit to Black Mountain, North Carolina. Ronald had informed us of his move to the community, and we happened to be passing by this past April on our way from Pennsylvania to see our grandchildren in Auburn, Alabama. Tammi and I spent one magical night in Black Mountain, visiting the Black Mountain Center for the Arts to watch Ronald's solo performance *LET IT BE ART! Harold Clurman's Life of Passion.*

Ronald's performance that evening, and probably every evening, was phenomenal. He became Harold Clurman for ninety minutes of storytelling, laughs, and tears. It was a history lesson about the theater in New York City, but the message was contemporary and in the moment.

The next morning, we met Ronald for breakfast and had a lovely conversation over coffee and sustenance. We exchanged gifts, neither of us expecting anything from the other! We handed over a box of books "on the house." He reciprocated with a painting of a bright, lovely landscape he had just done. He mentioned he had been painting his whole life, and I commented he was a "man of many talents."

On our way to Alabama, Tammi commented about the energy in Black Mountain, North Carolina. It had a positive vibe that was pervasive. We did a little research while driving and realized it was minutes away from the Billy Graham Training Center and numerous other metaphysical sites and organizations. Clearly, something spiritual is afoot in the area.

Then, not long after, Ronald proposed a book concept to include his poetry and art. At this same time, I had been contemplating a new imprint for the company: Lucky Shoe Press. The URL was available, and I reserved it. I added another logo to the many Sunbury Press imprints. Upon seeing Ronald's concept, we decided it would be a fantastic lead-off for the imprint in the region, capturing the energy of words and paint in artistic expression. Ronald humbly agreed.

As a former art gallery owner and current art collector and historian, I was immediately drawn to Ronald's paintings. Generally, the color palette and light are ebullient, conveying a love for life and the keen observations of a world traveler. The style is post-modern, post-impressionist. Some now refer to this genre as Open Impressionism (see Erin Hanson): a brighter, more colorful evolution of Van Gogh and Cezanne. Works like "Fisherman of Montevideo," "Ode to Edwin Booth," "At a Bridge," "When Peace Comes," "The Marsh in May," "Along the Tennessee," "Mecca of the West," and "Swayambhunath Temple, Kathmandu" are strong representations of this style.

One in particular, "A Chimney Alone," captures the serendipitous dichotomy of nature on a late summer day as a meadow engulfs the remnants of an ancient homestead. In summary, all of Ronald's paintings have energy, motion, and a strong spirit. They are life enjoyed.

Regarding Ronald's verse, it is experiential and sometimes performative in its shape. He expresses wonderment and appreciation for the natural world, as seen in his paintings, honoring the powerful evidence of creation all around him. In "Miracles Abound," Ronald writes:

> The gift is the moment.
> It's all we have.
> In all its splendidness—giving without asking
> anything in return.

Ronald reminds us that if we open our eyes, breathe the air, and bask in the sun's rays, we experience the joys of life from which we are often distracted. Ronald's work beckons us to live in the moment and experience these joys with him.

Yes, Ronald Rand is a "man of many talents." Some refer to such people as "Renaissance Men." In all of his work, Ronald demonstrates the gifts of a polymath: on stage, on the page, and on the canvas. I suspect the next "performance" will be a tranche of symphonies he has composed, ready for orchestral performance! I would not be surprised.

—Lawrence Knorr, Ph.D.
September 2025

Introduction

Writing poetry happened to me at an early age, influenced by all the rhymes and fairy tales read to me by my mother and late-night stories of the old west by my father, as I laid my head upon the pillow at night before I was whisked off to dreamland.

Isn't that where a great deal of the mystery of who we are resides? We're complex beings, much like an iceberg that reveals a tip of itself.

Poetry has helped me to try to make sense of it all, as I've traveled along the byways of life—growing and healing, revealing myself to myself and to others.

My mother would read poetry to me: Thoreau, Emerson, Whitman, Keats and Frost, Longfellow, Dickinson, Langston Hughes and Blake.

Many a time, she would recite by heart Browning's words from "Pippa's Passes." Even at 97 years of age, I would hear,

> ". . . The year's at the spring; And day's at the morn; Morning's at seven; The hill-side's dew-pearled; The lark's on the wing; The snail's on the thorn: God's in his heaven—All's right with the world."

Much later, I would discover Rumi, Kerouac, Ferlinghetti, Angelou, Ginsberg, Brooks, Plath, Akhmatova, and Mary Oliver; and today, poets such as Jaki Shelton Green, Joy Haryo, Amanda Gorman, and Billy Collins have touched my soul.

How does something capture my imagination and become expressed through a dance of words? This happens in the same way that a painting occurs for me.

Ever since I was a child and chose my artist's name—Ronjay—impressions would gently find their way into the climes of my consciousness, giving way to an explosion of form and color. Many times, these impressions came to life when I would paint on bark, shells, stones, and glass, expressing my joy and delight of nature and all the emotions swirling around me in the moment.

It reminds me of when my friend, Tim Stevenson, a master painter of the South, said to me, "I want to learn how to paint laughter." I believe we all have the ability to express our delight by letting our creativity come alive, even if we may not think we have that ability. I see it come alive in my workshops when we share storytelling, improvisations, and poetry together. Everyone's creativity bursts out in the most natural way. Think about that the next time you tell a story to a friend.

That's why every day is so packed full of miracles. Now, I have the pleasure to share another miracle with you—this book, and I hope you enjoy it,

—Ronald

A Beginning

The Marsh in May

Past the Spanish hanging moss,
the languid air tingles
with a not-so-readily apparent excitement
from the nearby crashing waves of the Atlantic,
above the dry, seemingly endless marsh
playing hide and seek between the cedar and the pine.

My view lingers and falls
on half-hidden crustaceans seeking refuge
from the foreboding heat settling
over every branch, twig, and bark.

Tracing against the cerulean, blue overhead,
the totem-like splintered trees arch upwards,
questioning their place, ever present,
but barely,
from the pounding jet stream
that comes and shapes all things,
leaving its mark for all time everywhere.

Are those gaping, screeching seagulls passing overhead
on their way to visit a junk
from China?

Or perhaps, a rambunctious hulk adrift at sea?
I do not know, nor should it matter.
Harbingers—drawn to the sea, cautiously curious,
carefully selecting one direction to go in,
wherever their travel may lead them.

Heading back, I turn one last time
gazing at the winding, crestfallen blue-hazed,
yellow-green creases of the marsh constantly changing
its color according to temperature,
the sun's approach and descent;
and my eyes dancing across its surface, searching for a lost bend,
a solitary indention never seen before,
that lies in wait . . . and may never be seen again.

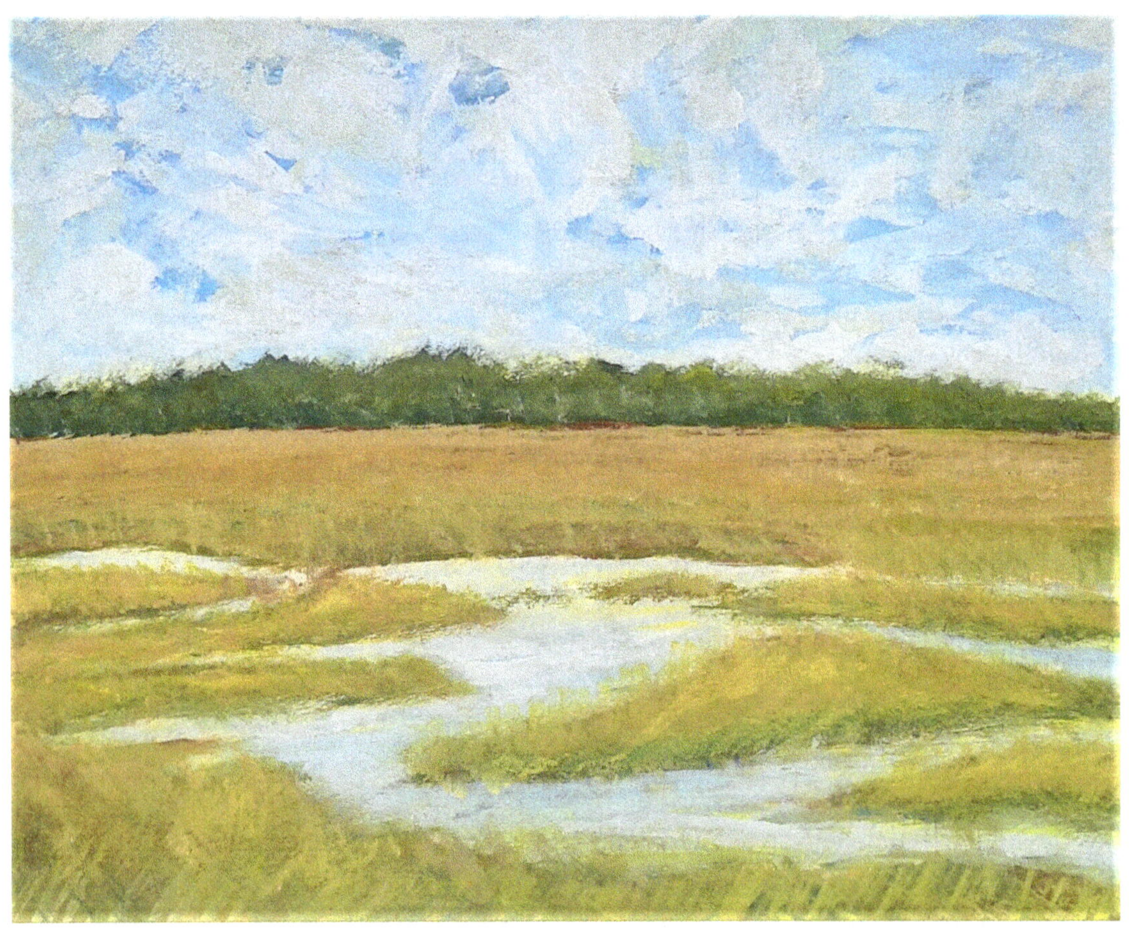

"The Marsh in May"

Fisherman of Montevideo

"The seas are rough," he thinks to himself,
"Still, they will bite my hook."

But the fish pay no mind. They stay where they are.

"Come to my long pole," the Fisherman says,
"Fish beneath the waves."

But the fish pay no mind.

In crash the waves, down the sun burns on his head,
as the wind blows.

"Fish, fish, where are you?" the Fisherman calls.

But the fish pay no mind.

"Never was like this," he thinks to himself, looking at his bucket.
"Always full by now."

The sun leaves its path on the waves, on his face.
Wiping his brow, a sigh comes to his lips.

A seagull lands.

"Do you know why?" the Fisherman asks.

In crash the waves, down the sun burns on his head
as the wind blows.

A blur of white, the Fisherman's alone.

"Fish, fish, come to my hook," he calls.
"When I was young, the fish came."

But the fish pay no mind.

In crash the waves, down the sun burns
on his head as the wind blows.

"Fish, fish, I must eat too!" the Fisherman calls.

But the fish pay no mind.

In the distance, the sun fades.

Bowing his head. "Fish, fish, you are my only friend."

In crash the waves, as the wind blows.

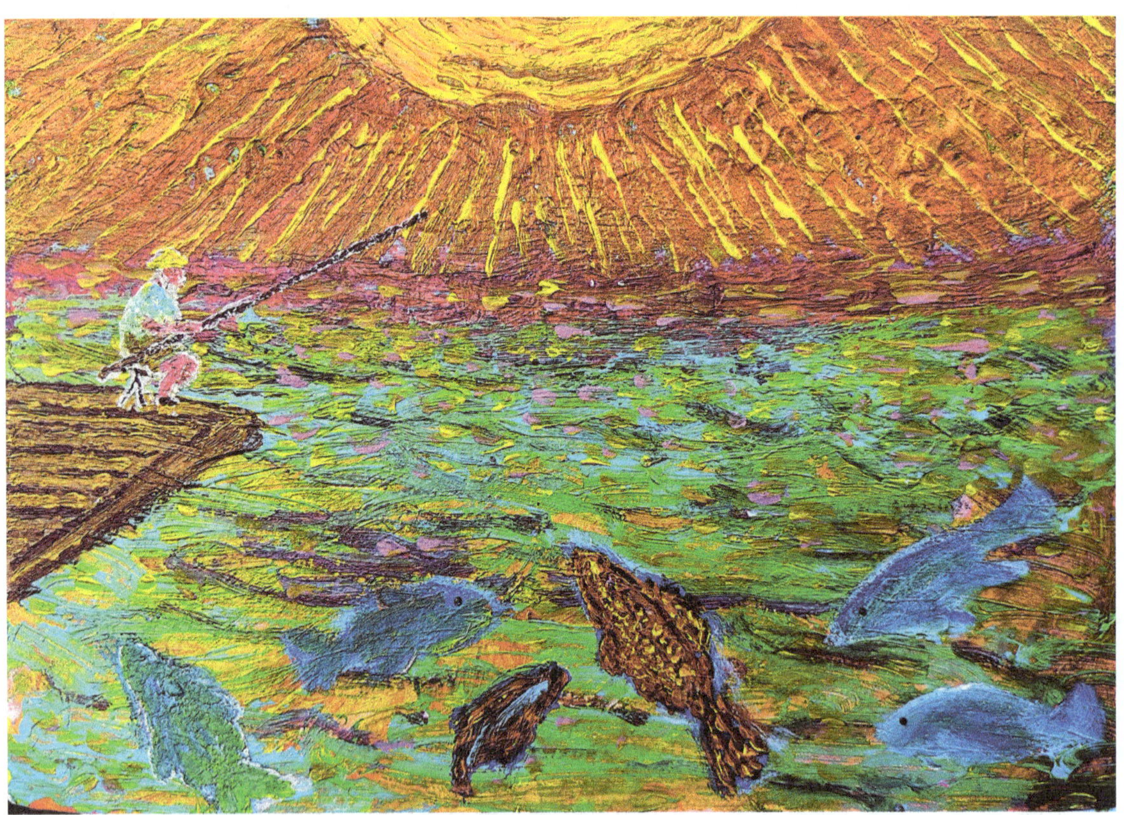

"Fisherman of Montevideo"

Shall We Call You—Tree!

If not for your roots
which wander everywhere stretching to infinity,
we would digest you like we do everything else
and soon forget you.

Hold us firmly rooted to this revolving sphere.

Outstretch your tentacle-like limbs upon this earth,
your blossoming eye-opening specters of green
fluttering and unfolding in every direction,
beneath an all-encompassing soaring canopy of blue.

Or so we believe it to be.

In fact, it's not even a distant cousin,
but our eyes have no choice
but to see what they see.

Without them, we would live in a darkened existence
unaware of the rich panorama being played out before us.

Around me, the crisp wind tickles
the moment-ago still leaves,
which now dance with glee
shaking upon their benefactor's limbs
stretching out from a wizened monolithic trunk,
as thick as the columns of the Parthenon.

You are home for so many, carrying ages within your fibers,
your membranes, your furrows, your roots announcing to the world
Tree!
Standard bearer of time—past and present.

Gliding swiftly by, an uncomplacent hawk swoops
towards the nearby mountain, and I hitch a ride
to climb, to soar into the sky beneath the
placid harmonica-shaped clouds streaming by.

Ever-present, the moon and stars
watch over our charades.

Puppets and puppet-masters alike,
we shake sticks at the Gods,
playing games to hide our true intentions
in our haste towards our eventual demise.

Our mumblings, our rumblings cannot hold a candle to you—
Tree!
Center of the universe.

As we revolve from light into darkness,
and then back again into light.

As if that would allow us to see more clearly.

If only we could trust our senses,
we could listen to see the truth,
and calm our soul
to find a way forward.

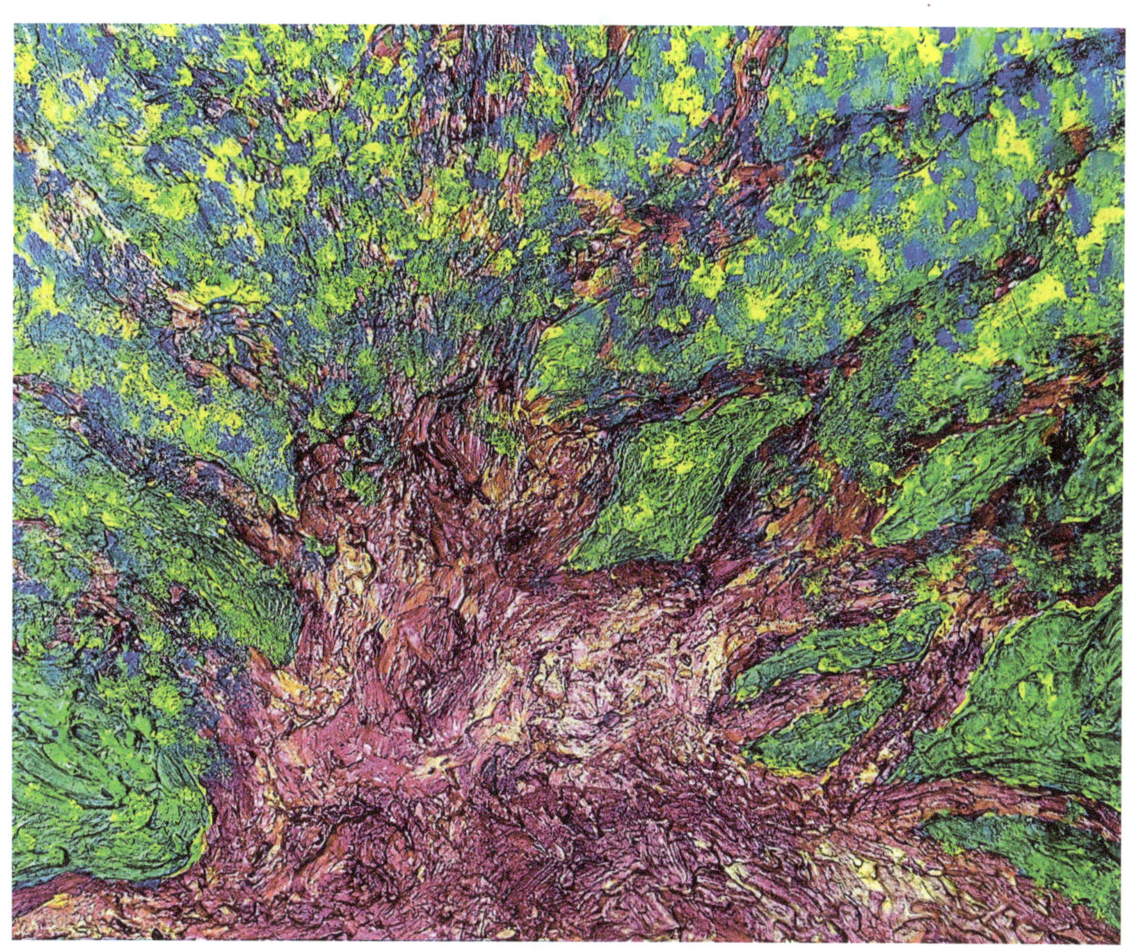

"Shall We Call You—Tree!"

Ivy Green

Beneath the perdurable stars, nestled between
 honeysuckle and magnolia, surrounded by
 dogwoods, roses and ivy,
 a simple clapboard house stands.

In a small town in the South.
 Deep, deep in the South.
 Alabama, to be exact.

And you might ask what town it's in,
 where it resides, and I'd be happy to oblige.

After a chief, Tuscumbia, they named their town.

And there came a day, when a Captain and his wife
 crossed their threshold . . .
 and history was made.

Keller was his name, and they had a daughter.
 Helen was hers.
 In fact, they had several children.

But to this one solitary soul, the Good Lord said:
 "You will see. You will hear. You will speak."
 But only for a time.

 Then darkness came.

She went this way. She went that way.
 She went every way she could.
 Searching. Groping. Grasping.
 But that world would not let her go.

Finally, the Kellers brought a young woman named
 Annie who understood.

"Teach her," they said, "Teach her, for if there's one thing
that'll save her, it's knowing she's not alone."

So, Annie did.

But the key to her soul was still locked inside, unknown.

One day at a black well pump, Annie tapped
into Helen's wisdom's well,
and Adam's ale crossed Helen's palm.

And lo and behold—meaning came.
"Wa—ter!" "Wa—ter!!" "Wa—ter!!!"

Yes, a "miracle worker" changed Helen's life that day.

And it all began beneath the perdurable stars,
nestled between honeysuckle and magnolia,
surrounded by dogwoods, roses and ivy's bouquet.

In a small town in the South.
Deep, deep in the South.

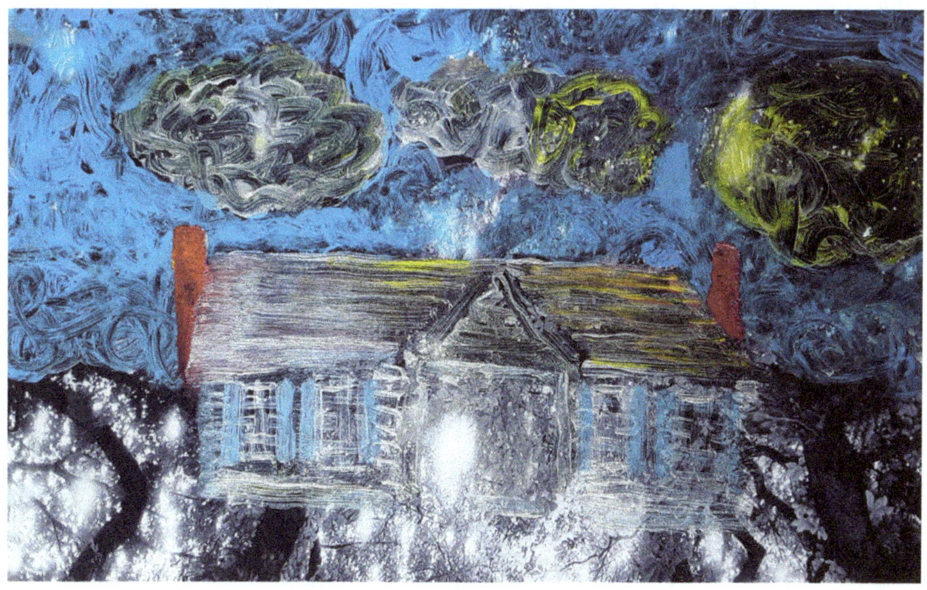

"Ivy Green"

In the Distance a Trumpeting Comes

Low

at first,

as if the approaching

welcomes a whole nother world

of wonder.

Bursting overhead

comes

a band of feathered friends

loud as a Hosanna-singing chorus.

My heart leaps!

Harbingers of swiftness break the air,

shooting straight as arrows

lifting higher, racing faster

into the distance

blaring!

Catching my breath,

I pause and thank the heavens above

for such a sight

of grace and

delight.

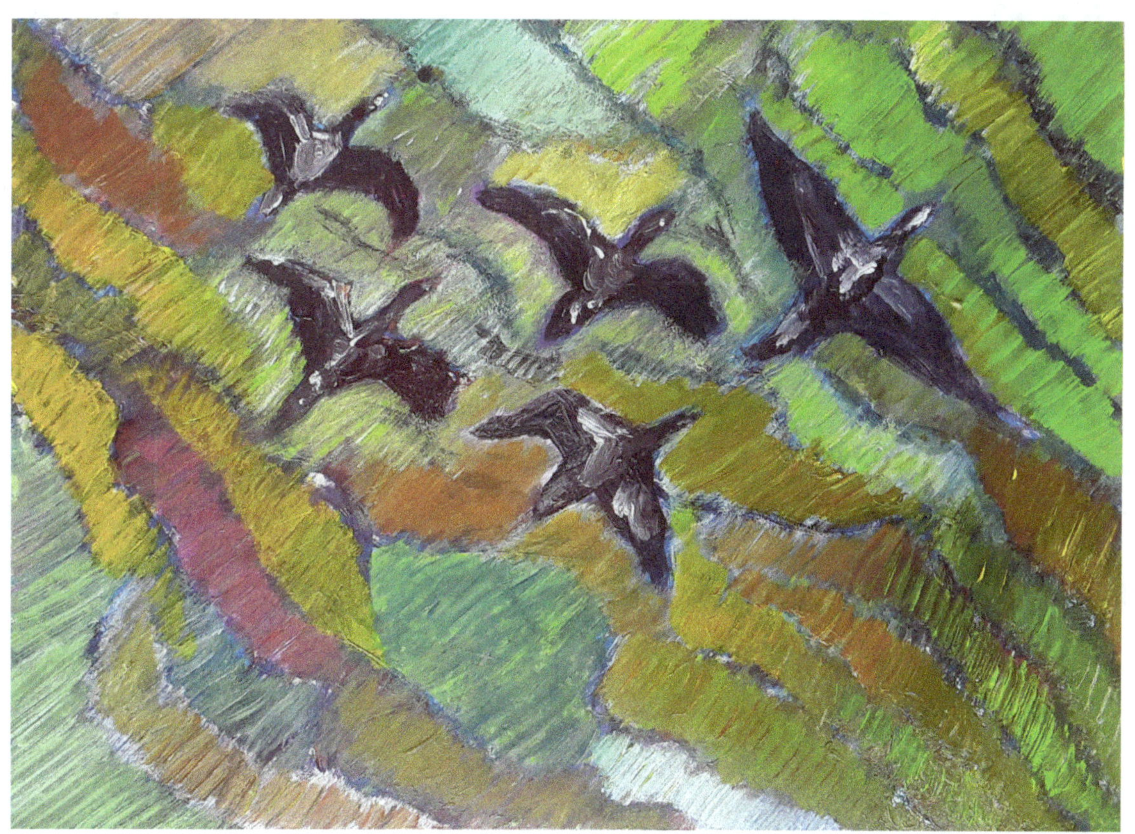

"In the Distance a Trumpeting Comes"

Ode to Edwin Booth

Among the poplars and the birdcalls,
he stands in the park, silent and immovable;
his gaze almost impenetrable.

Still . . . I hear him whisper of ages gone by
when giants once bestrode the earth.

"I stood upon the stage and through me
Gods spoke; I was but a vessel
for all that is human.
For all our petty comedies,
and our impassioned woes."

Across the park now his quiet room still remains;
and upon a dusty shelf his 'Yorick' skull.
Nearby his quill and facing them;
a portrait of his Mary, and his will.

Before his shrunken bed his fragile slippers sit;
nearby his often-read-from Shakespeare,
unopened and unread.

If you could but know dear blessed Edwin,
how all that you began continues on.

Then your heart would truly fill
and rejoice beyond compare.

To witness all the beauty and the life
now residing within your blessed home.

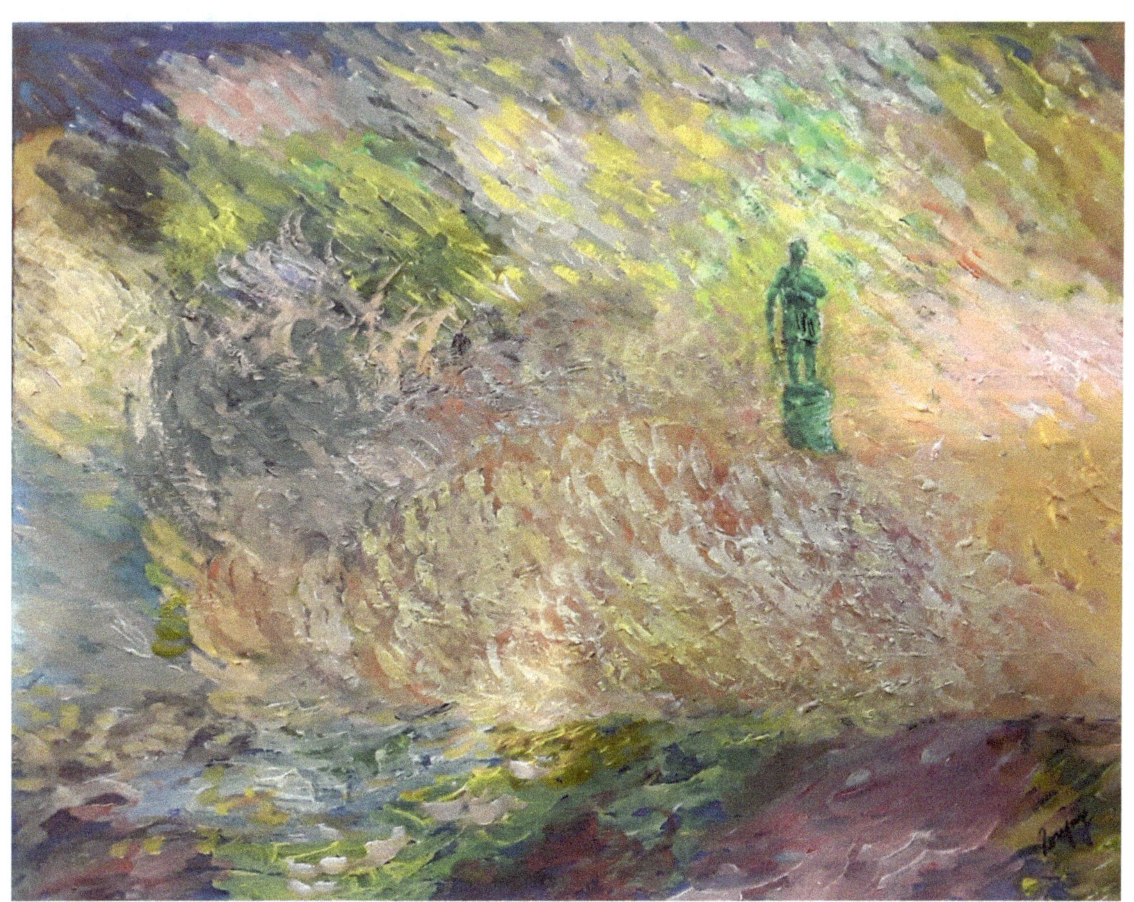

"Ode to Edwin Booth"

Charlie Chaplin Dances

Stars in my sky-soul light the way forward.

Oceans of heart, liver and brain
call forth memories of who I have become,
of what I remain.

Submerged, I break the surface and play
among timeless excuses, inexorable questions.

As still water heads towards the sea.

Lining my brain kaleidoscopes, reflections of
unease knot the inside of my soul.

Yesterday was so full of hope: fresh and alive.
Now images go screaming to the sky.

I hear: "Speak up! The truth will set you free!"
Did Gandhi know more than me?

Once high in the Tortolitas cave dwellers
carved into stone where water was scarce
among the saguaro and the pine.

Perhaps there is another time, another face, another form
that will align with all my hopes and dreams.

The fertility gods fish and cast their newly spun
web, entwined, intricately layered by a miracle-maker.

Are we no less designed?

Trapped by time, yet completely free are we.

I close my eyes and watch topsy-turvy visions
of Charlie Chaplin dances.

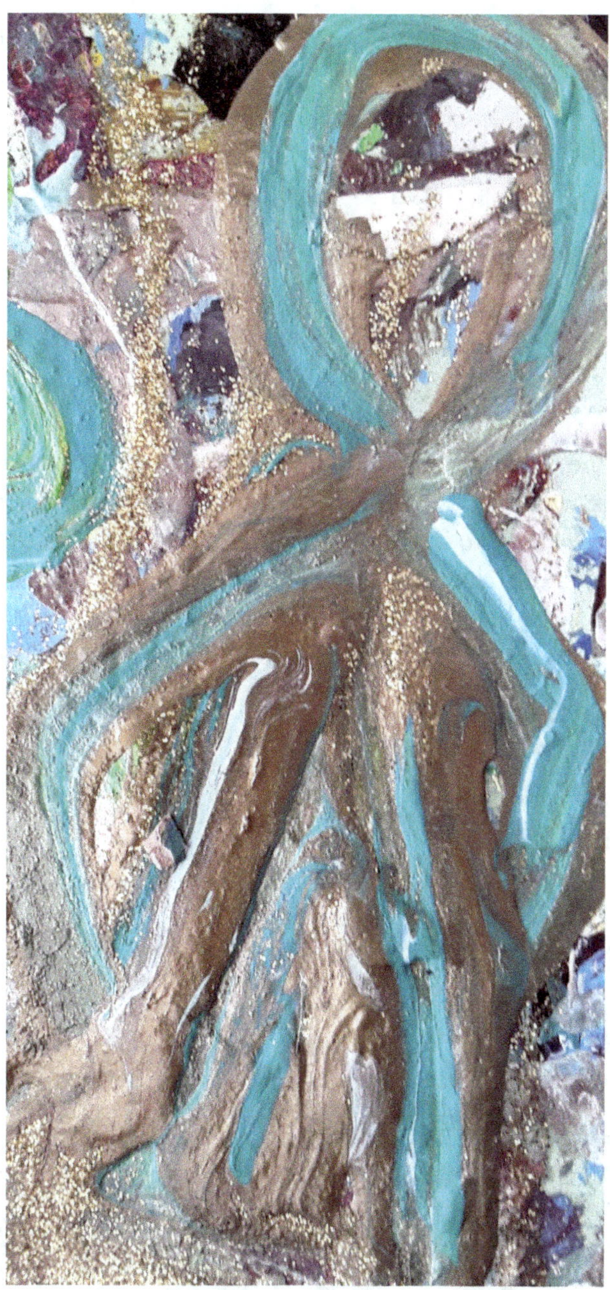

"Charlie Chaplin Dances"

Olympia

Before the pillars, my eyes follow their gaze to a mountain top
in the distance, that those who came before me, too had looked upon.
Around me the stones still speak.
I gaze upon their gaping wounds left from the ages.

Only	I
a few	of
pillars	this
remain	age.
of a	They
temple	of
for Apollo.	theirs.

Yet . . . the same sun beats down upon my head, as it did upon theirs.
Here where the Olympics began, worshipping at this temple.
I bow my head to say a prayer. What do these pillars think of us?
Life has changed in so many ways. And it will again.
Yet . . . somehow these stones remain—to tell their story.
Some how they stand. And I bear witness to their age.

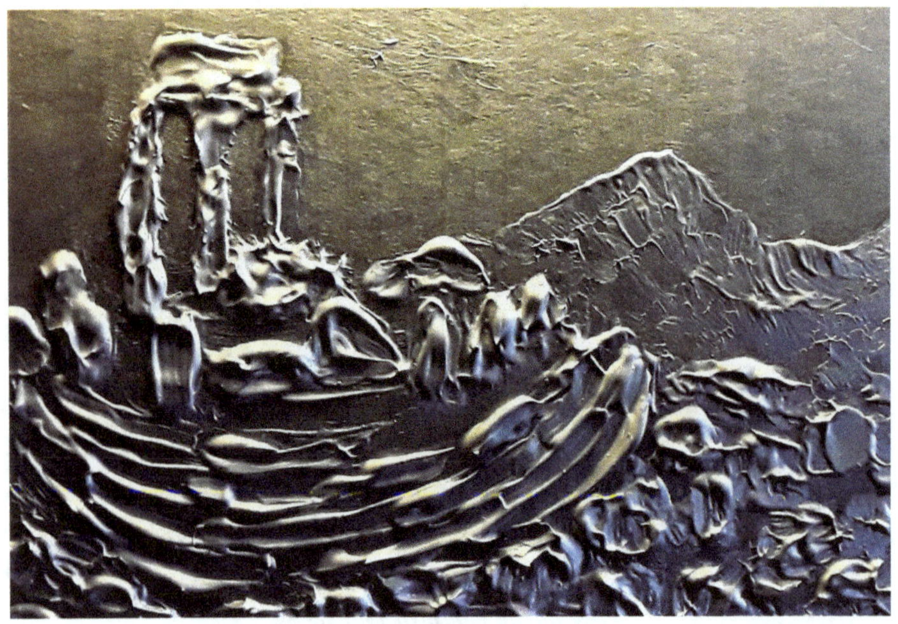

"Olympia"

Stepping Forward

Swayambhunath Stupa, Kathmandu

Floating at the top of the world
echoes surround me,
cymbals clash in the air.
Alive to the moment,
the smile of the sun licks my head.
The gong of life dances in the breeze.
Forget all worries, it says.
You alone hold the key to your destiny.
Sleep a thousand dreams and
awaken on your path.
Clear your mind.
Open your throat.
Sing like the hawk.
Dance in the sky.
In the air what do you feel?
Peace. Joy.
The gift of life.
Horns blare.
Join in the celebration.
Monkeys chatter, looking on from roofs.
Monkeys chatter inside my mind.
Let them go!
Let them go!
Let them go!
It is why you have come.
Rest. Replenish. Renew.
The smoke clears.
What do you see?
Coconuts. Peacock feathers.
Taste when you are ready.
Touch when you are ready.

Smell when you are ready.
Hear when you are ready.
Bow your head. Step inside.
Your time has come.

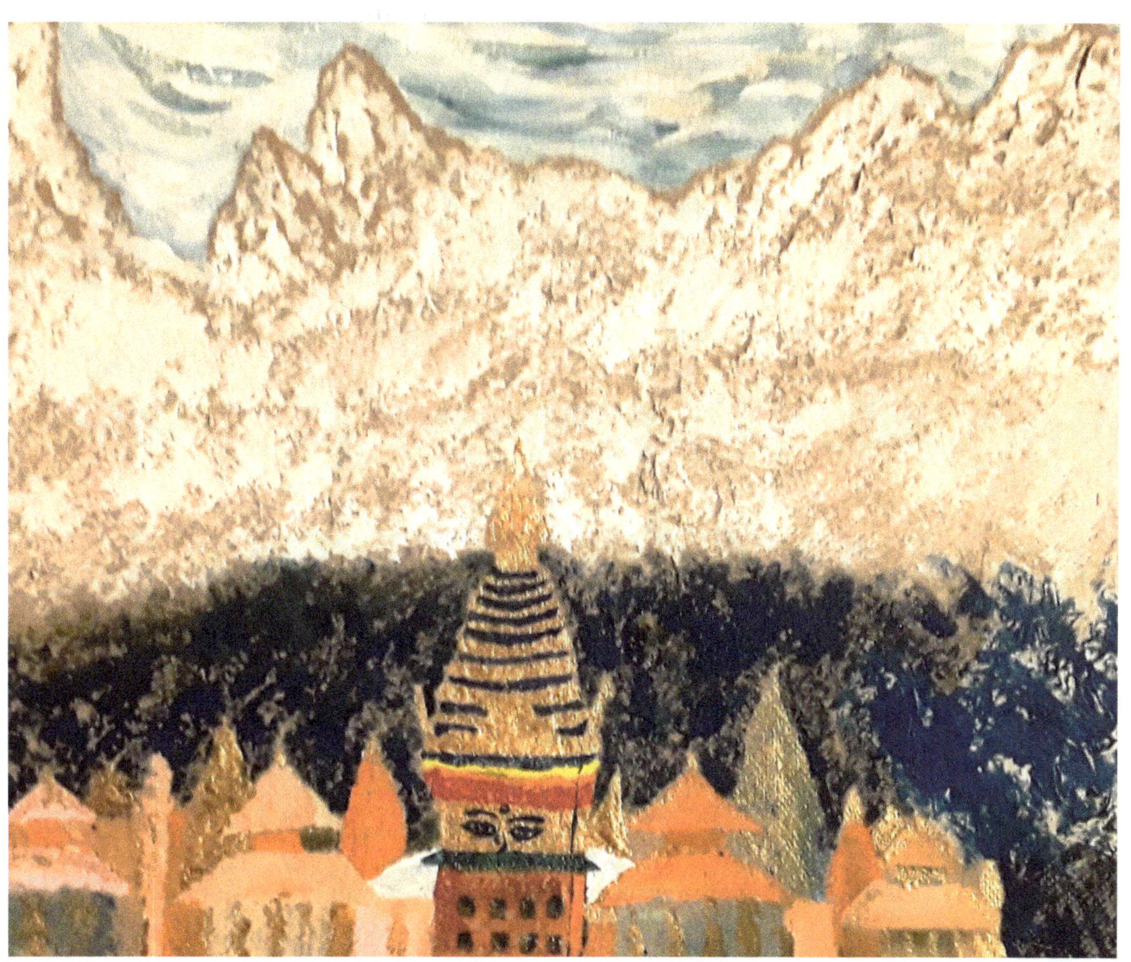

"Swayambhunath Temple, Kathmandu"

Ode to Jean-Claude Van Itallie

Walking nimbly like a leprechaun
among the brambles in a fading light,
Jean-Claude whispers to the earth,
while reaching up and pulling down a withered limb.

"Catch me if you're nimble enough,"
you seem to say,
"Before I slip behind this branch, that bush.
I'll lift off
and rise into the sky,
surrounding all with my embrace."

His steps, sure and steady,
glide forward, one at a time,
in an 'all-knowing',
past watching statues of ancient civilizations,
speaking a tongue neither seen nor heard.

Love was your watchword,
while all around your light,
shined brighter for all the world to see

They say the world was simpler once.

How soon we forget the Siege of Rome,
the destruction of Jerusalem,
the lines of young soldiers shackled to sand,
scanning the horizon to be rescued.

The countless ships, one that held your family,
that tumbled to their fate in the bowels
of the North Atlantic during a war,
a war that was fought to end all wars.

Upon one ship rode a young boy,
fleeing the marauding tribes of darkness,
inching his way forward,
towards the brighter shores of freedom.

Where once arrived,
unleashed his spirit
in a singular breath of time.

I can still see your shining visage
facing me in your sculptured apartment,
smiling, all aglow,
even in the face of so many adversities,
so many struggles,
so many pains.

Still you smiled.
Still you laughed.

You were a witness.
Reminding others,
"I have seen."

Keep searching, Jean-Claude.

Yes, always keep searching.

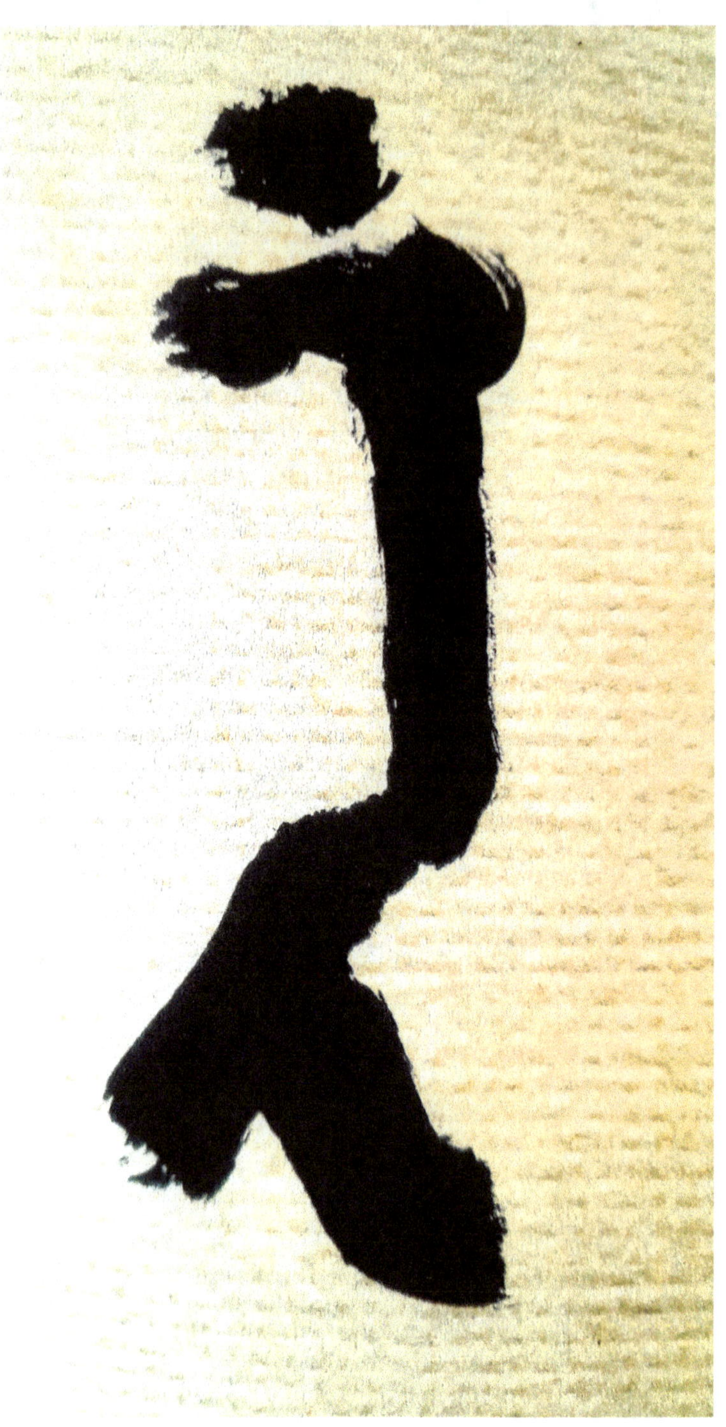

"Dancing Man" by Jean-Claude van Itallie

Across the Ages

The climb had been steep through the wind and the rain.
With offerings on their backs they came—with bison, deer and bear.
And as Sirrus disappeared,
each entered the cave, aware of the task at hand.
They knew the cave held life; rituals to be obeyed
or they would never see the light of day.
Stones were placed as markers as they moved
forward, further inside the cave.
While above their heads, the chamber danced,
glittering from the flames they carried lighting their way.
This was where the herd would be.
Setting down their loads, first animals were
sacrificed, then splintered for their use.
And when it was time, they lifted their voices,
calling forth the herd.
For above their heads they clearly saw what would appear.
Between the dark stone, their fingers chipped into the cave,
shaping forms, outlining beasts upon the clay.
They pounded stones, as they pounded bones.
In the dim glow, a crimson buffalo appeared.
Soon another, until the whole herd was born.
And when they were done, they prayed,
and ate, and rested.
While above their heads, dancing in the lime,
a herd pounded the earth
for all eternal time.

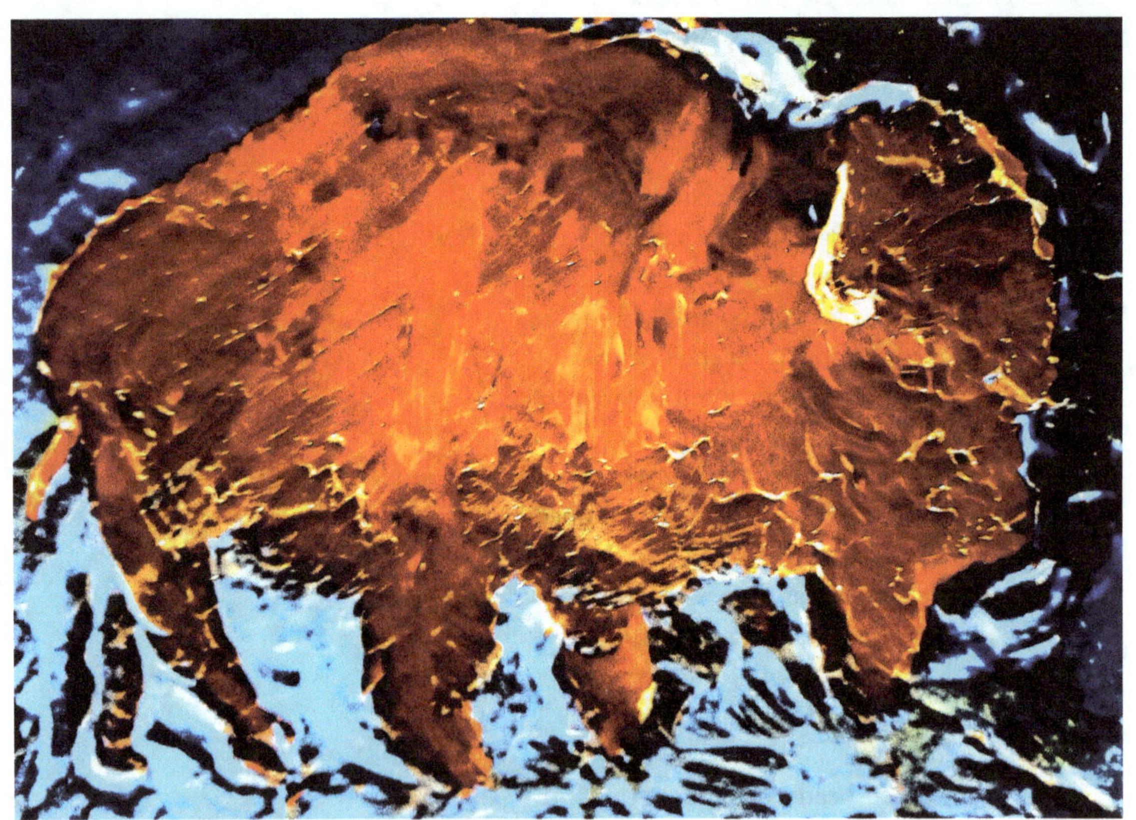

"Across the Ages"

Mostar Peace Bridge

Ancient stones arching through space—Tell me your story
Emperor Suleyman the Magnificent ordered
Mimar Hayruddin, "Build me a bridge across
the mighty Neretva but if it falls, you fall."
And so, Mimar began building.
"Build, Mimar, build for your life," the people exclaimed.
And up went the bridge.
This in 1566.
And as he built . . . he dug his grave.
The bridge reached and soared, but would it stand?
Would his life be sparred?
For four hundred and twenty-seven years
the stones held, blessing all who crossed.
While battle upon battle was fought upon its pedestals.
Stand, mighty bridge, stand!
Connector of all people,
Muslim in the east,
Christian in the west.
Stand!
But lo, a new blast of war came.
Turn away, Mimar, turn away!
As stone upon stone falls into the mighty Neretva.
This in 1993.
"Take us out!"
the stones cry out submerged under the water.
"Though we are mere stones, we carry your peace!"
So, the people listened.
Up went your bridge, Mimar, with your same stones.
"Walk again upon us," they say.
"But never forget, each step carries
your courage, your love,
your peace."

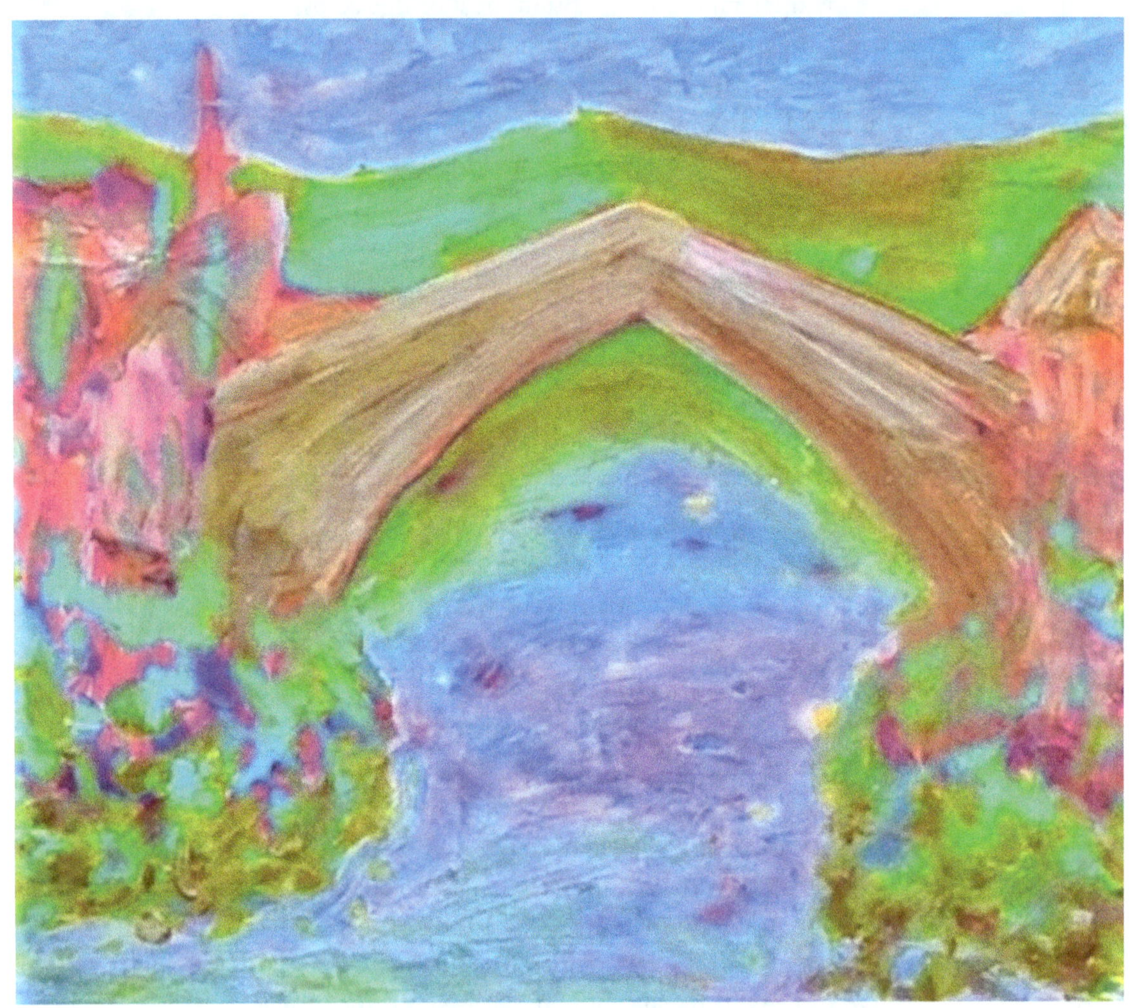

"As I Step Out on Mostar Bridge"

As Angels Watched Overhead

A man is at work, a son of the South.
A woman is at work on the man at work,
    a daughter of the South.
What is his trade you may ask? Her trade?
Both honest trades, both born to create.
Artisans at work.
Yes, we've stumbled upon artisans at work.
                                        As Angels watched overhead.
Both work, as the spirit works through them.
She goes about her business with faith,
    and a knowing of the brush.
He tends to the wood, bending it to meet his needs.
While the man in the painting holds a skirt of wood.
She speaks the language of paint holding a brush of wood.
                                        While we are but witnesses.
This man, this solitary man, meets his wood.
This woman, this solitary woman, meets her canvas.
Both suspended in time and space,
    fashioning art from life, upon a solitary planet,
    beneath the stars of time.
They say art can soothe the soul.
Music lifts the spirit, both bringing everlasting life.
But first, wood must be fashioned,
    strings attached, paint mixed and applied.
Born with a gift of seeing,
    the artist's hands fashion a painting through a craft,
    springing from a soul of light.
As she gently dipped her brush into the colors of the earth,
    she listened and observed.
Thus, the music of the canvas was born.
There is that moment when true inspiration comes.
When Mozart played, Einstein's brain flashed.

This painter beheld a simple act of creation,
and now her light illumines the world.
As Angels watched overhead.

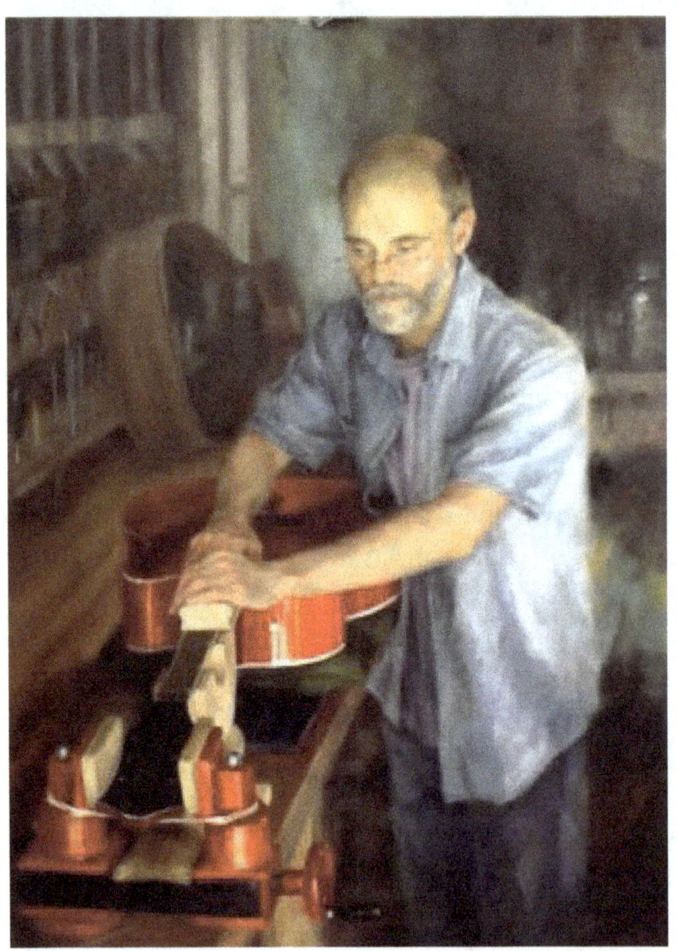

"The Luthier" by Martha Carpenter

Born to Fiddle

As a child the waters sang to him
    feeding his musical soul.
So did his desire for a fiddle and a bow.
Tucked away in his room, he practiced day and night,
    his dreams dancin' with delight.
And as all things are in this world meant to
    be—he fiddled, as one sister painted, another
    magically sewed, a third, played Bach,
Beethoven, Mozart, in every mode.
His fingers swam across the strings, like
    the onrush of a cascading sea to shore.
Puttin' the devil to shame so he'd never
    come near Georgia no more.
Spirits would lift hearin' "Amazin' Grace,"
    soothing souls and hearts that needed to
    soar.
A fiddler can take us many places from
    a plaintive pasture to a peaceful tale.
Dipping low into our hearts, flyin' us high
    to a palace back on down to a pail.
One thing's for certain though,
    this young feller was born to fiddle.
To brighten lives with his bright passion,
    and unassumin' grace.
Now he'll just keep on a fiddlin' till all our
    cares are gone—and all that's left is a smile
    shinin' on our faces, and in our soul.

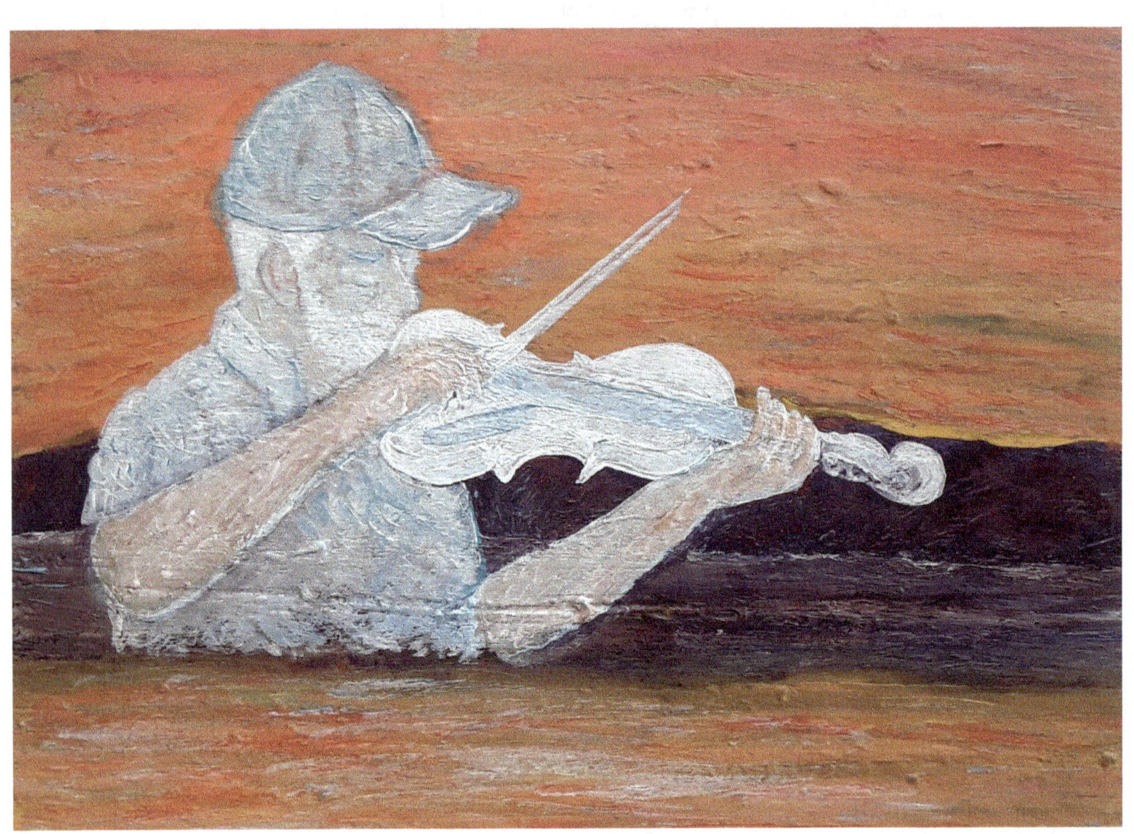

"Born to Fiddle"

The Heart Knows

Through the trees, the sunlight bursts forth, while the breeze dances,
swaying upon each twig, each branch.
There is only acceptance and gratitude for this moment.

Catch the day in all its rareness.

And even though waves may dash upon the shore, and lightning crash.
Know it soon will pass—giving way to a newer time.

Let peace come into your heart.

Allow yourself to begin anew, allowing all sorrow, pain and regret
to drift away upon the tide.
The only answer is a willingness
to accept this new day in all its grace.

To see as far as you can see.
To hear as clear as you can hear.
To love as fully as you can.

With this new day, let forgiveness fill you as you swim towards the light.

Let the sunlight touch you, bursting through the trees.
Let the breeze dance and sway upon you.
Step forward . . . knowing everything is possible.

Let peace come into your heart.

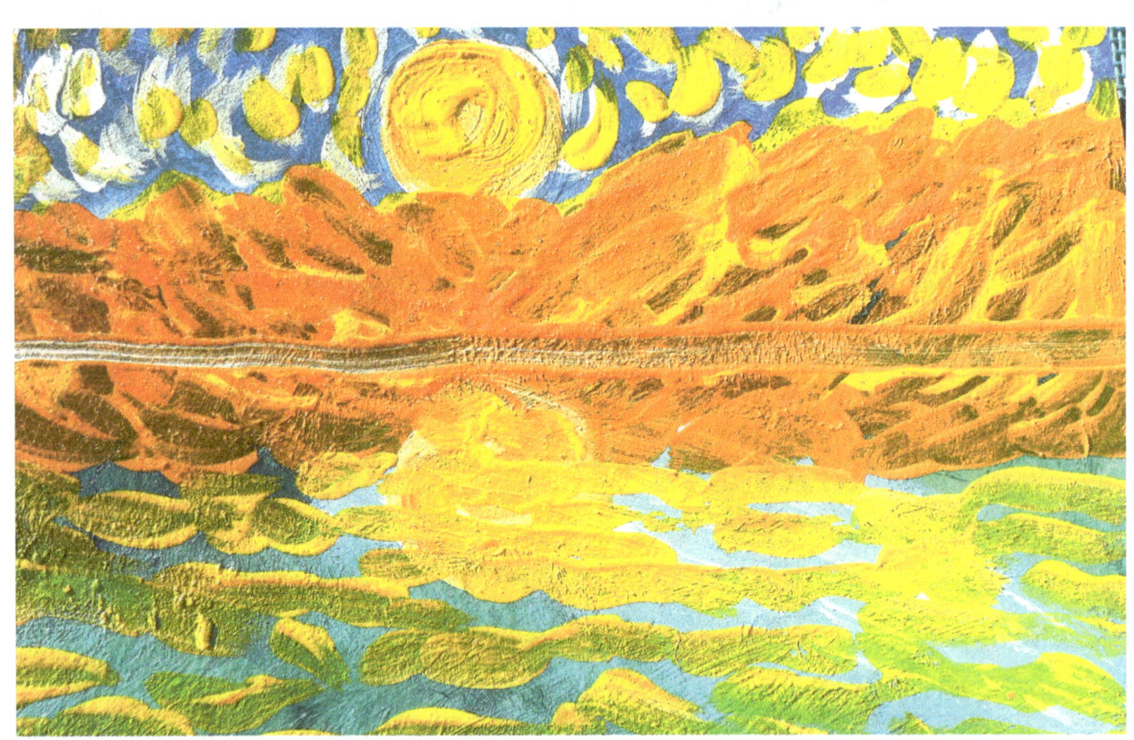

"When Peace Comes"

There Comes a Moment

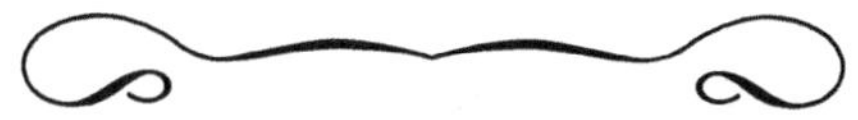

Leave a Trail

Indigo sky above.

Glaciers like marble, and hanging ice fields
stretch in every direction.

Pristine expanses of frozen snow
endless to the horizon.

Soaring to the sky, snow-capped mountains
hold their white-flecked spruce trees
tightly to their chests.

Snow flies up like dust in the wind.
All is serene.

. . . except for the howling of the Alaskan Huskies,
relentlessly pushing forward.

My mind thinks on Emerson:
"Do not go where the path may lead,
go instead where there is no path
and leave a trail."

Like a needle in a haystack,
the sled and I hurtle forward.

Glittering colors of the tundra swimming by

All time and reason swallowed whole.

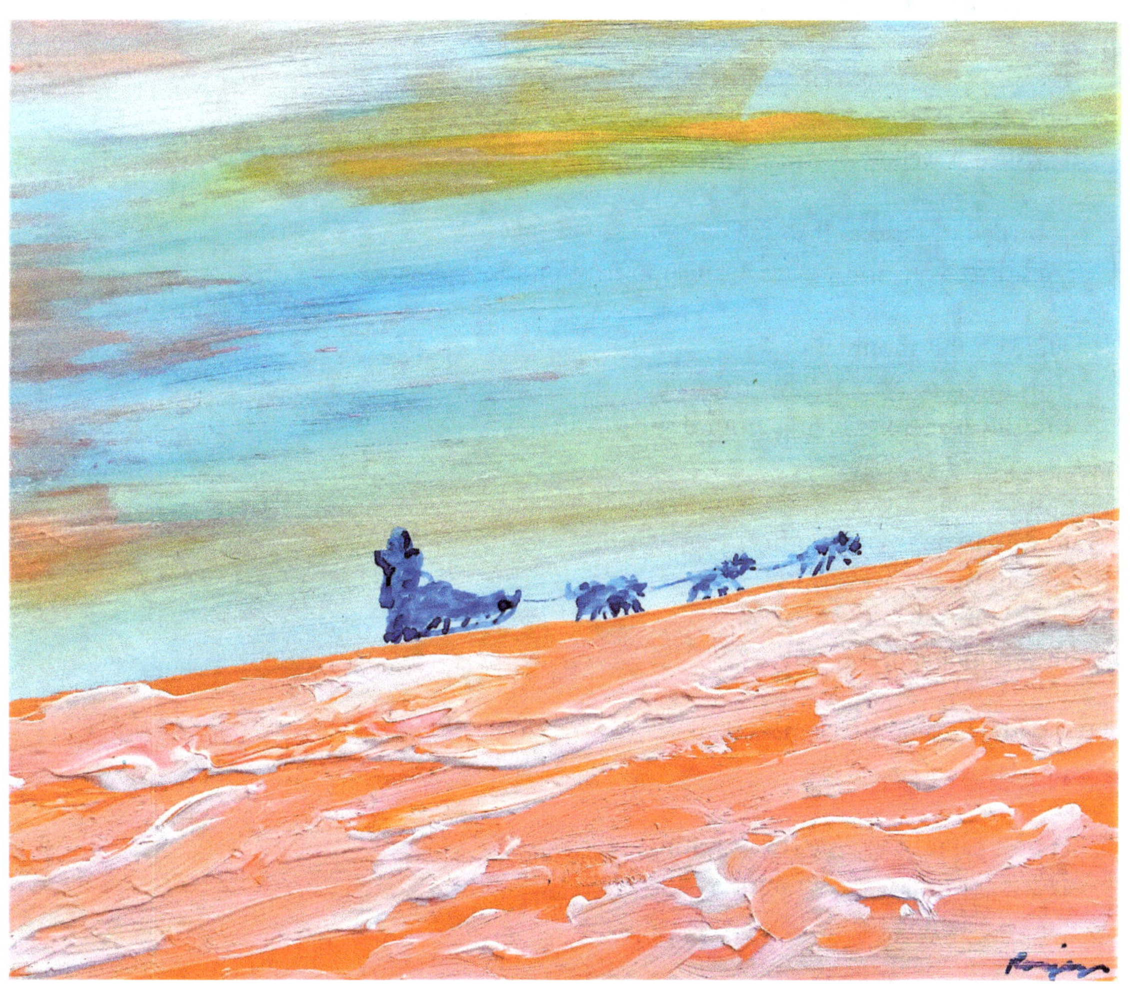

"Leave a Trail"

A Deer Came to See Me Today

It came down the hill and seeing me it stopped,
and slowly made its way to where I sat.

It stamped its paw as if to say hello.
Friend or foe?
I wished it well and sent my love its way.

It turned its head as if to say:
"Yes, I see you, and we are in this moment one."

Here on this mountain.
This morning.
On this planet, revolving around the sun.

A deer came to see me, and time slipped by,
as we gazed into each other's eyes.

I see you. Yes, and we exist
in this moment as one.

Ah, the breath of recognition,
of peace and love.

A deer came to see me this morning
It seemed as if we had found one another,
and everything before had brought us
to this moment.

Then turning away, it suddenly stopped.
Glancing back, it's eyes seemed to say,
"Don't you know who I am?"
And then was gone.

That is what life is.

One moment leading to the next,
slipping through our fingers,
like strands of gossamer,
while we find a way forward.

For, in that moment
we saw one another . . .
and that is how to live.

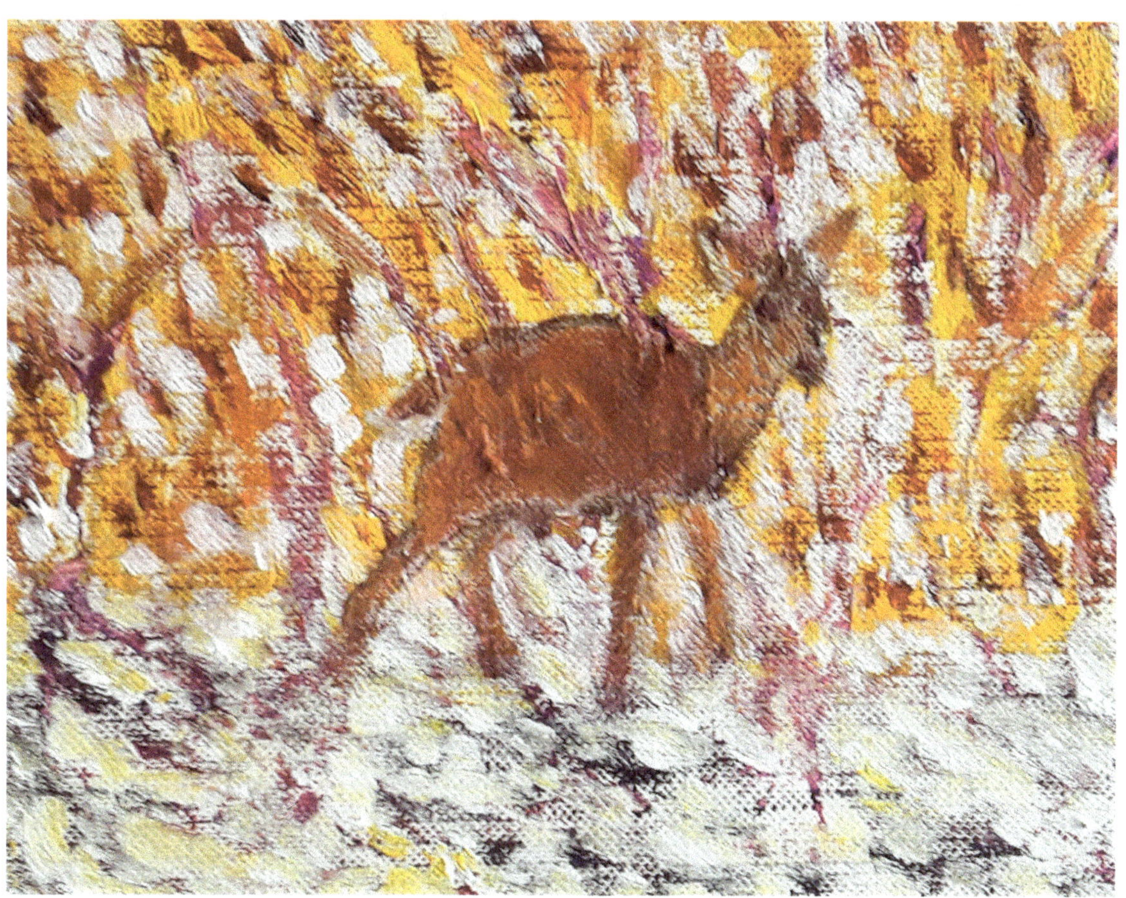

"When a Deer Visits"

Around the Bend

Around the bend
dancing fog on the river
swirls, dissolving into air.

Birds' reflections pass by
through the trees.

Sunpockets catch
the morning's arrival.

Proudly standing among the willows,
a long golden beaked heron
waits.

Time slips away.

Brambles of tomato vines
past their prime
taste the coolness
knowing another season
has arrived.

Life happens all the time.

Around the bend,
a bird is calling
to my heart.

I slip out of my skin and fly.

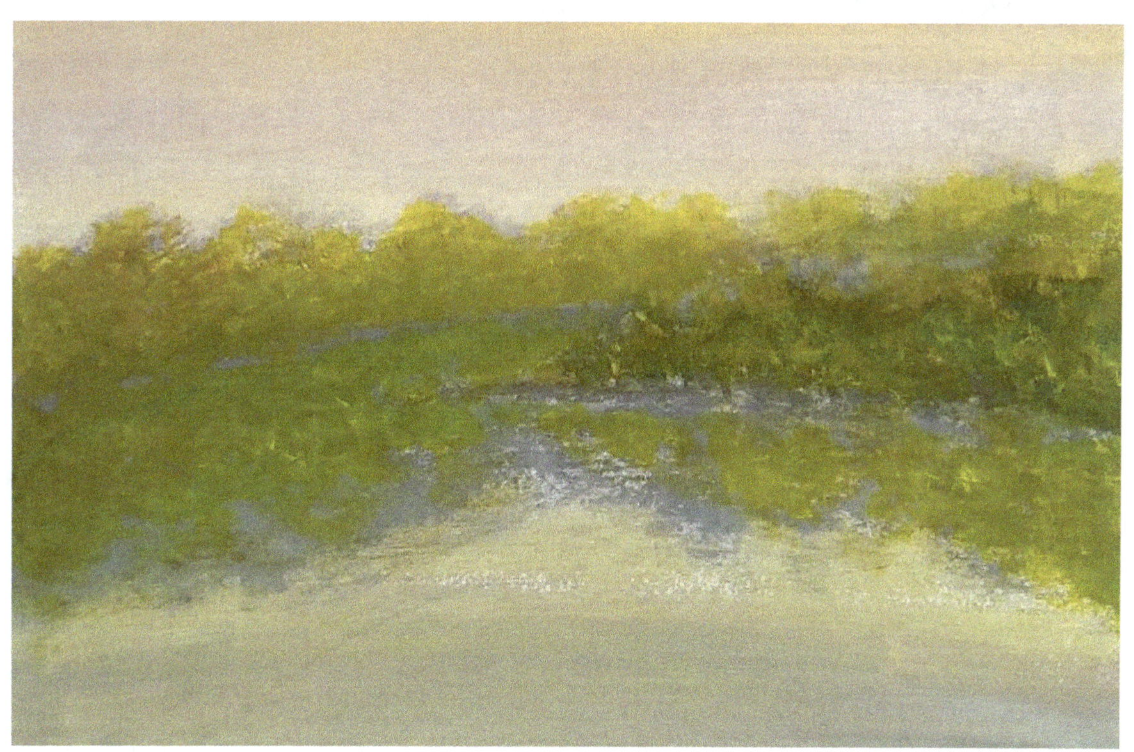

"Around the Bend"

Ode to My Mother

The bare trees outside are no longer strangers.
They know their way to the sky.

"Come with me," they say,
"We are there for you."

Sometimes resting, sometimes reclining,
sometimes silently swaying,
entwined in an unseen world.

Other times noticeably they touch,
perhaps reminiscing of times gone by.

Stretching outward, I see their climb,
their route taking them to the sky,
through space, even beyond . . .
to infinity.

How can I remain earthbound
when I have such friends as these?

A different world . . .
than where my mother is.

Inside a world . . .
held gently.

A world alone . . .
now that her eyes have closed.

A sigh escapes my lips.
My mother's eyes now see . . .
another world.

They used to see this one,
    the one she loved so dearly.

A world of trees that clothed
    the deer that would come
    beneath the branches,
    outside her window.

That would light her heart up with wonder . . .
    with delight.

Turning their heads,
    standing stock-still,
    their eyes would peer deep into her soul.

And her fingers, with brush in hand,
    would slowly paint these deer,
    emerging from beneath the trees.

Now within her, their image remains.

Their glances, as they turned their heads,
    stopping to bear witness
    under the low-lying limbs of life.

She still sees them . . .
    or so I believe.
Under the trees with their watchful gaze,
    beneath the azure sky.
"Follow me," they seem to say.
    "Let us go for a drink together along the creek,
    beneath the winding curves of the trees."

And so, they would go.
    beneath the curving trees,
    much like the fragile fingers
    of my mother's hands.

The creek, the trees, her fingers . . .
    are all chilled now.

As chilled as the air outside.

One moment her eyes opened,
    a smile appeared.

A smile of recognition.. . . .
    for one brief moment.

And then all too quickly flew away.

Yet, still resides within my mind.

Like the image of the gentle deer
    that stood outside her window.

Like the tears I brush away,
    that now fall upon the painting
    she painted so carefully.

Now, the bare trees outside
    hold me in their sway,
    singing gently to my soul:
    "We understand."
    "We care."
    "You are not alone."

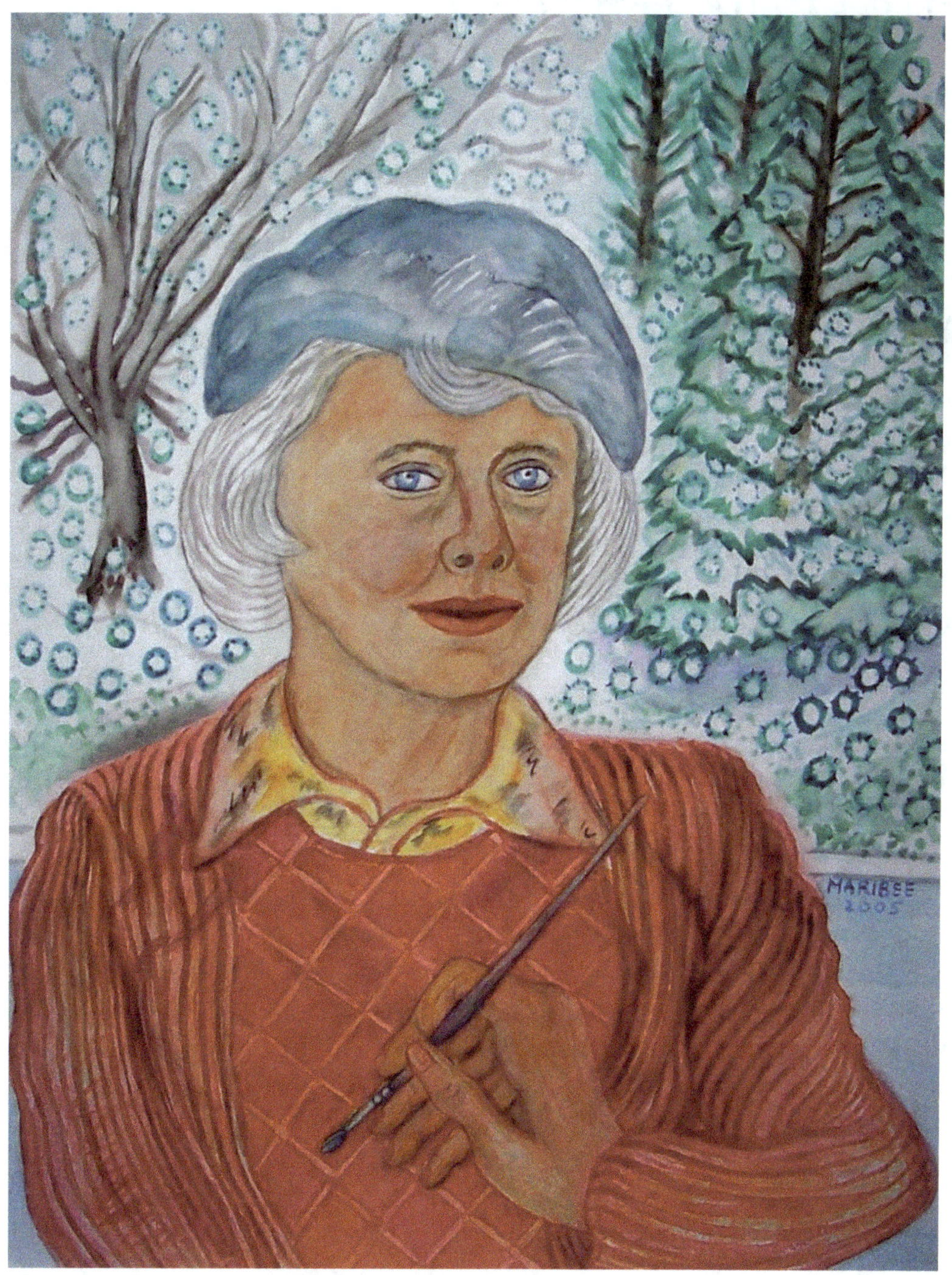

"Self Portrait at the Window" by MariBee

Along the Tennessee

While they fish along the Tennessee,
 new plants take root and sprout,
 through God's good grace across the land of the free,
 and the home of the brave.
Milk of human kindness, and a giving hand.
All alike are we on this glimmer of hope,
 hearts beating freely, oceans of dreams afloat.
Softly, softly blows the breeze,
 whispering among the trees.
While above, swirling tufts of white pepper the sky.
Singing a calming tune, the Tennessee laps along the shore,
 having meandered its way from its mouth.
 Splash!
A catfish does its "air dance" in the sky.
Nearby a heron, still as a statue,
 darts a glance in its direction.
A moment later, almost motionless,
 the heron bends towards the water.
Still bending even further,
 until it's almost one with the surface . . .
 Splash!
Quick as a jackrabbit, the heron flies out of the water,
 a wriggling catfish between its beak.
While the meandering Tennessee calmly flows by.
All it takes is a leap of faith,
 for miracles to take place.

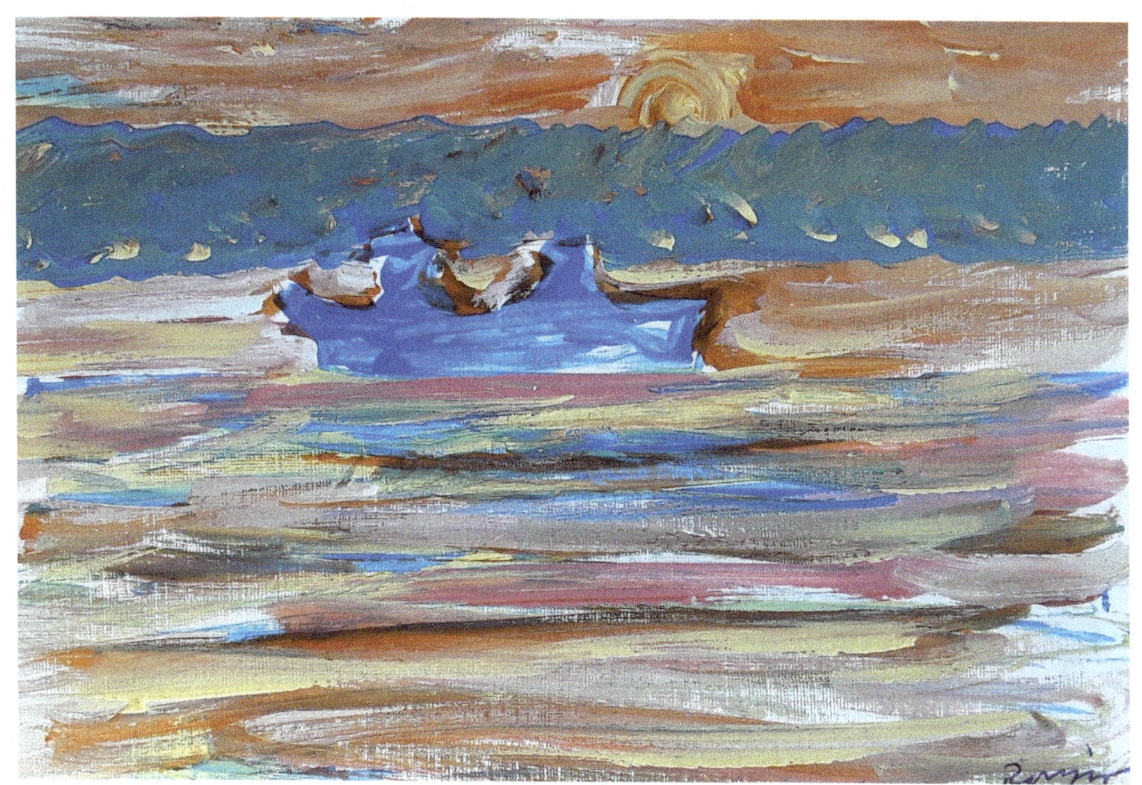

"Along the Tennessee"

When the Sky Turned Black

Like peaceful hippos in a row, battleships and mighty man-of-wars
rest in their berths, idling in the morning dawn.

While deep below in their berths they rest . . .
young men dreaming of arms around them,
and those they left behind, of home, and apple pie.

Then comes a roaring, from behind the burning orb.
Then comes a roaring, from above, like never before.
Then comes a roaring, whistling down, ministers of death.

And as the huge behemoths shudder and gnaw,
with nowhere else to go, but down . . .
they twist and slide into the fiery deep below.

Those who can, as heroes do, rise and fight
against the raining death.

But with destruction all around and no place to hide,
it's over before it's almost begun.

That fateful morning, when the sky turned black.

The water is calm now. Waves find themselves
gently to shore—in peace.

Yet, bubbling up from down below . . . oil rises,
reminding us of that fateful day.

To never forget our heroes and to hold them in our hearts.
December 7th, 1941.
Today the bugle sounds.

The flag flies at half-mast, reminding us
of those who served their nation.

A duty claimed by the courageous few,
because they stood for country,
for liberty, and for peace.

But sacrifice is never easy. It comes with a price.
Those willing to lay down their lives
so we can live ours.

Remember that morning, that fateful morning.

When the sky turned black and never let go.

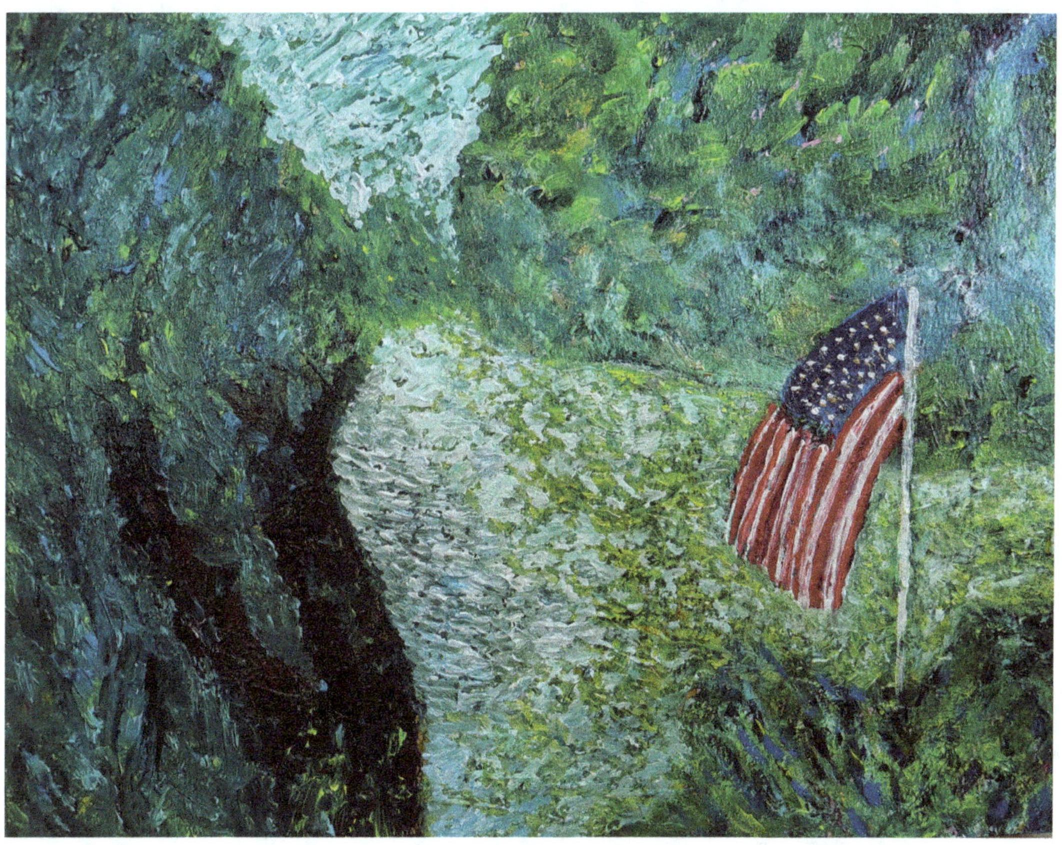

"Still Standing - Still"

In Walks Time

In walks time, wriggling its way between the tightly wrapped chocolates
in their shiny plastic wrappers.
In between the unselfish onions sitting comfortably in a basket nearby.
While outside, a fisherman's hook dangles beneath the waves of the lake,
beneath the leaden sky.

Standing in the shallows, a motionless heron waits,
while my soul flies up and down with Mozart's cascading notes
swimming across the room, inserting themselves between my ears,
and my thoughts of time.

I wonder . . . how do calla lilies survive the frost?
How long will we be able to survive on this planet?
Who stopped to see the first dawn?

A colorfully painted bookmark by Tim rests gently between two pages
inside a new book, "The Dig," that came in the mail.
Without a care in the world, it saves the spot I need to return to.
The pages waiting for me to resume.
My mind waiting for me to resume,
in anticipation of how the story will unfold.
How different will it be from the film I have been watching?
How different has the writer captured life in letters,
weaving them together to remind us how to live?

There is never a right way or a wrong way to live,
except the right way and wrong way we know to be true in our hearts.

Knowing that each moment counts.
That each day . . .
We have a chance to start all over again.

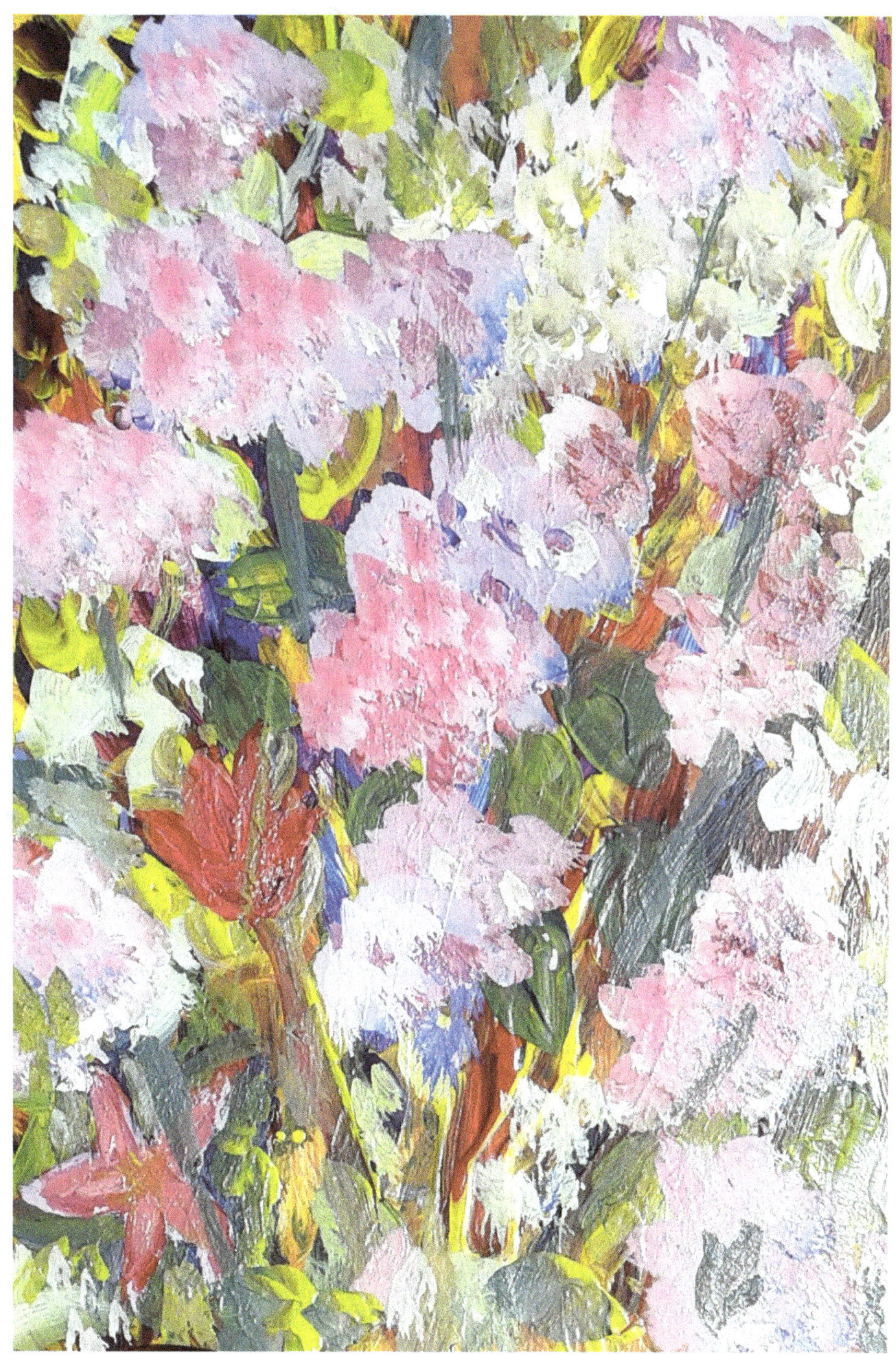

"Moment of Grace"

Athens of Africa

Across the uneven cobblestones I go. Bewitched, stepping through your "Arabian Nights" gates, losing all sense of direction and time. Winding my way through your labyrinth-like mazes of the Fes el Bali Medina. At every turn, the "call to prayer" echoes around me, through me, above me. My heartstrings played upon, penetrated, enticed by you. Fez, a city like no other. It's as if I have fallen, like Alice into a rabbit hole, squeezing through your crushing walls only wide enough to pass through one at a time. While above me, the Moroccan piercing blue sky stretches in every direction settling upon your lemon-yellowed walls of mud and line. Who are you—"Athens of Africa"? What mysteries do you hold close to your chest? The stifling searing heat of the desert air has long ago dissipated the coolness from the nearby Atlas mountains. Nor is there any escape from the insistent-clanging, clanging, clanging ricocheting through the air, the pounding, pounding, pounding upon copper pots and pans. I step nervously over elfin-like milky white kittens squirming, purring beneath my feet. Did you drop from out of the sky? Barrels of dates and olives, spices overpower my senses from the souks. I turn a corner, a camel's head and goat's head stare aimlessly—no doubt a delicacy beyond compare. There but for the grace of God go I. Before me the pounded gold-plated doors of the world's oldest library. Behind them, the first university on the planet. The doors part. I peer inside—a mosaic tiled courtyard of seemingly endless intricate geometric patterns of blues and browns greet me surrounding a silent marble fountain, no longer sprouting fresh cool water. My eyes swim, dissolving into plastered walls covered in sutras from the Koran, a sea of swirling Arabesque patterns of Islamic calligraphy, flowing one letter into the next. A donkey ambles by, its hooves clopping, clopping, clopping, a seller of wares aboard. Pigeons quickly flutter aside, shadows of wings caught in the glowing haze, and I am swallowed by a city hidden behind white painted barren walls. A pungent smell grabs my senses. Voluminous round stone vats brimming with dyes of blue and red, yellows and brown fill my eyes. Children scurry over the Chouara Tannery soaking hides of camels and goats and cows in urine, pigeon poop, and quickline, before being transformed into leather. Quicly I cover my nose with mint leaves from the smell. Why had I come here? What drew me to Fez? Why feel as if I've fallen off the face of the earth? I am but an inhabitant of this planet for just a short time. For one moment, my soul can take off and fly!!!

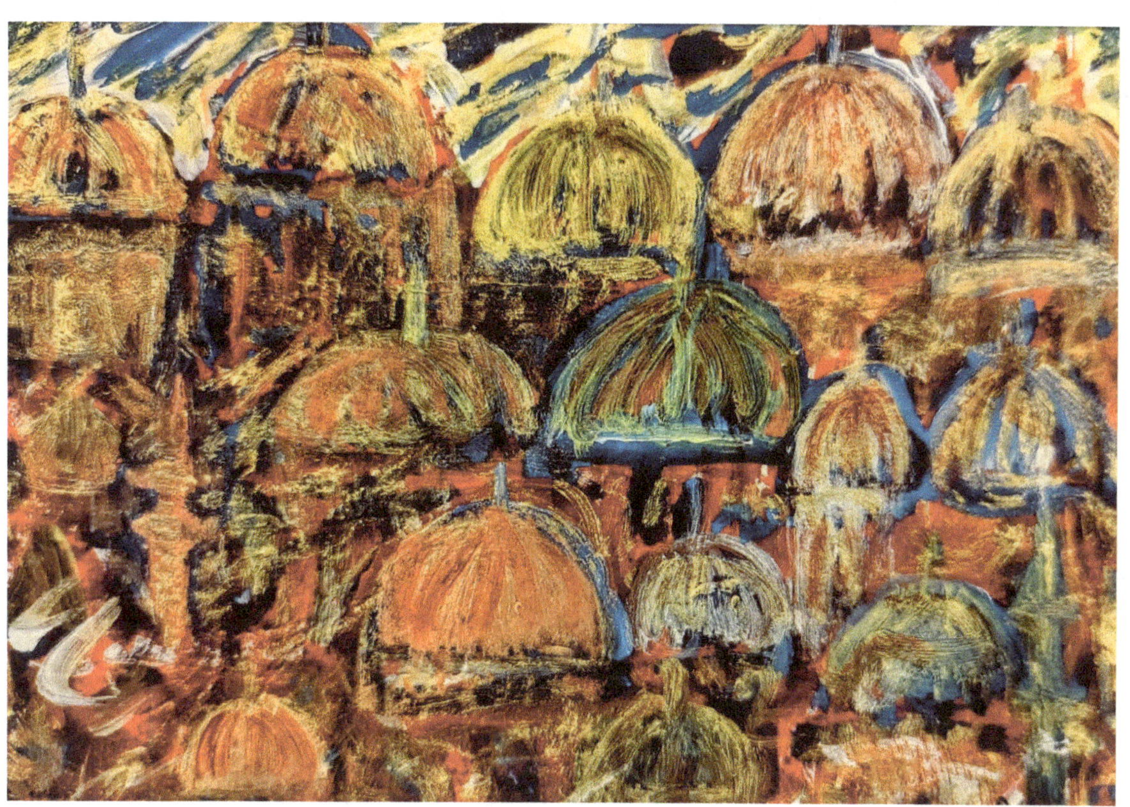

"Mecca of the West"

At a Bridge

I stop at a bridge resting comfortably on the earth.

Nearby the trees look like they reach all the way to the sky,
as we turn, without a pause, through space and time.

Somehow, the universe holds us in its warm embrace.

My eyes travel up the deep furrows of an oak and I
wonder . . . What were you like when you were just a seed
planted in the ground? Did you fall from another tree
and find your way beneath the earth to take root?

Just like we all do.
We seem to find a way to keep growing,
to sustain our lives each day.

For if we stopped—where would we be?

A woodpecker glides across the trunk of an
old standing being. How does it
not fall off? And just like that, it's gone.
I know it was there a second ago.

Did I see it?
Or was I sleeping and saw it in a dream?

Sometimes, I wonder why images come.
How we summon them? Where they come from?
What they mean and where they go?
Perhaps I'm just a figment of my imagination.

One day I'll wake perhaps on a different planet,
in a different body as someone else.
I'll speak a different language, eat a different food.

Chewing slowly, I'll try to remember
what my life was once like.
If I can.

All the things I once held in my hand are now lost—
gone forever, in a flood.

Floating down the river somewhere in my mind . . .
in a different space, in a different time.

I wave goodbye over and over again,
but for some reason, they don't wave back.

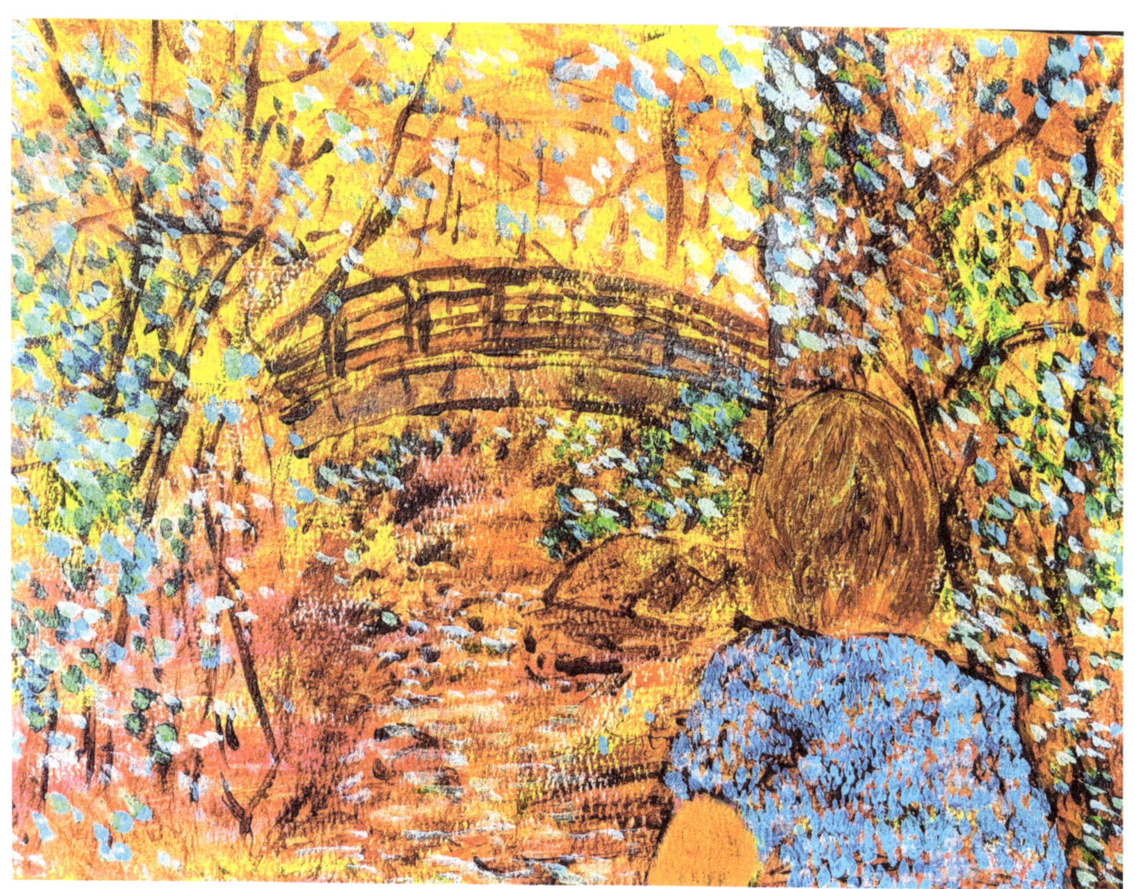

"At a Bridge"

Everything's a Gift

The Peak Awaits

Rising
majestically
the peak awaits.
All the summits
you have passed along
way, the crooked byways
and steady streams are long
gone. The ins and outs, the questions
that will never be answered in long-forgotten
caverns rattling around inside your skull no
longer exist. Now there is no going back. The only
route is forward. Forward! The wise souls who have
come before pointed the direction. Check your pockets! Toss
away all torn and tiny maps you have stashed in every pocket.
Jettison all etched sayings drawn in the sand. They no longer serve
you now. Only what you carry in your heart knows the way. Let go of
all memories. Stand tall and catch the dawn. Let it spread across your face.
The time is ripe for a deep breath. Is that the biggest smile you can muster?
Feel the glow. Every prayer you have uttered has been answered. It is time
to let go! Step forward to claim your destiny! It has been waiting for you!

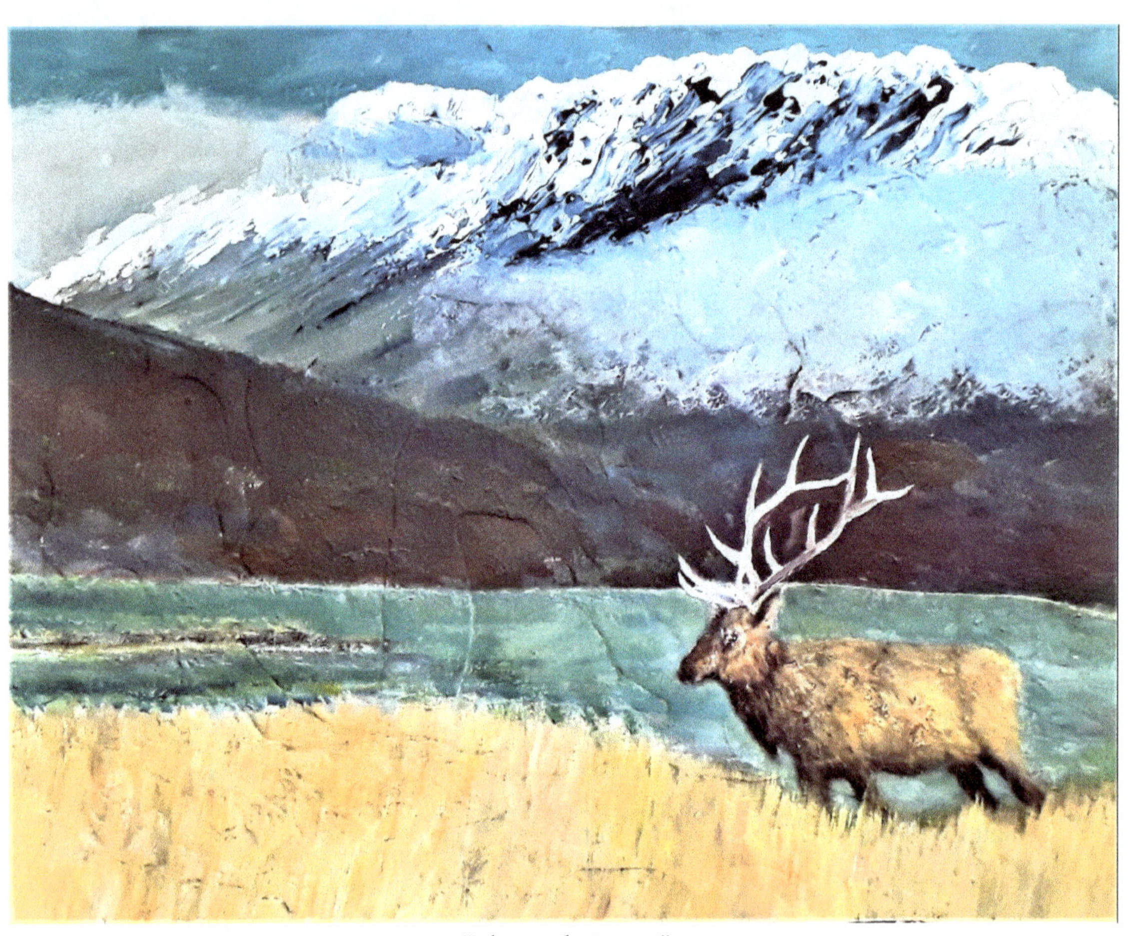

"The Peak Awaits"

Along the Rio

It is a far way to go to Paysandú
but we're almost home.

Hold on, just a little bit further.

At least, the priest at St. Benedict left us a few scraps,
and the Rio has not risen.

There is much to be thankful for.

When we return, you'll receive an extra ear of corn.

There will come a day when you and I will part.

You willl go your way,

I will go mine.

It is a fact of life.

I don't remember so well these days.

It is a good thing you know the way.

Is there anyone who hears my cries in the dark?

Am I the only one?

My eyes burn, but as long as I have air in my lungs
and you, my friend, are here . . .

Bless this day, and all that is good in the world.

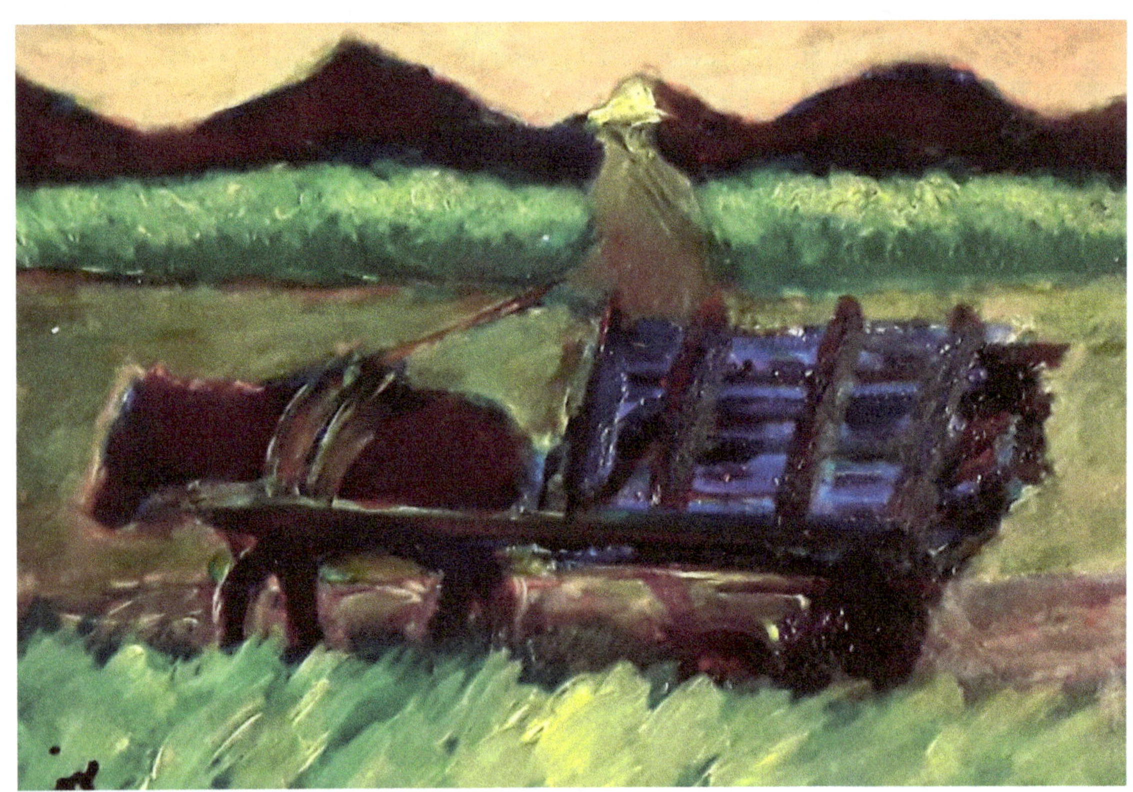

"Along the Rio"

Ribbons of Color

Ribbons of color speak to me through the trees.

While above owls and buffalo clouds stream by,
elephants and leopards charge,
and dragons spread their wings
to take flight over the mountains,
and keep going towards the dawn.

Close behind, cloaked in deep magenta,
the arching sun pierces through the
mist as we spin, like a wonderful top,
through the grace of the great Mystery.

Miracles abound, as long as we're willing
to open our hearts and accept the treasures
being shown to us.

I'm glad there are others like you and me,
who look upon this world with open joy,
and see the day as a gift.

And when I leave, I will return
to see where I have been,
to marvel at the dusk,
and laugh at the dawn.

Kiss the new day with your entire heart.

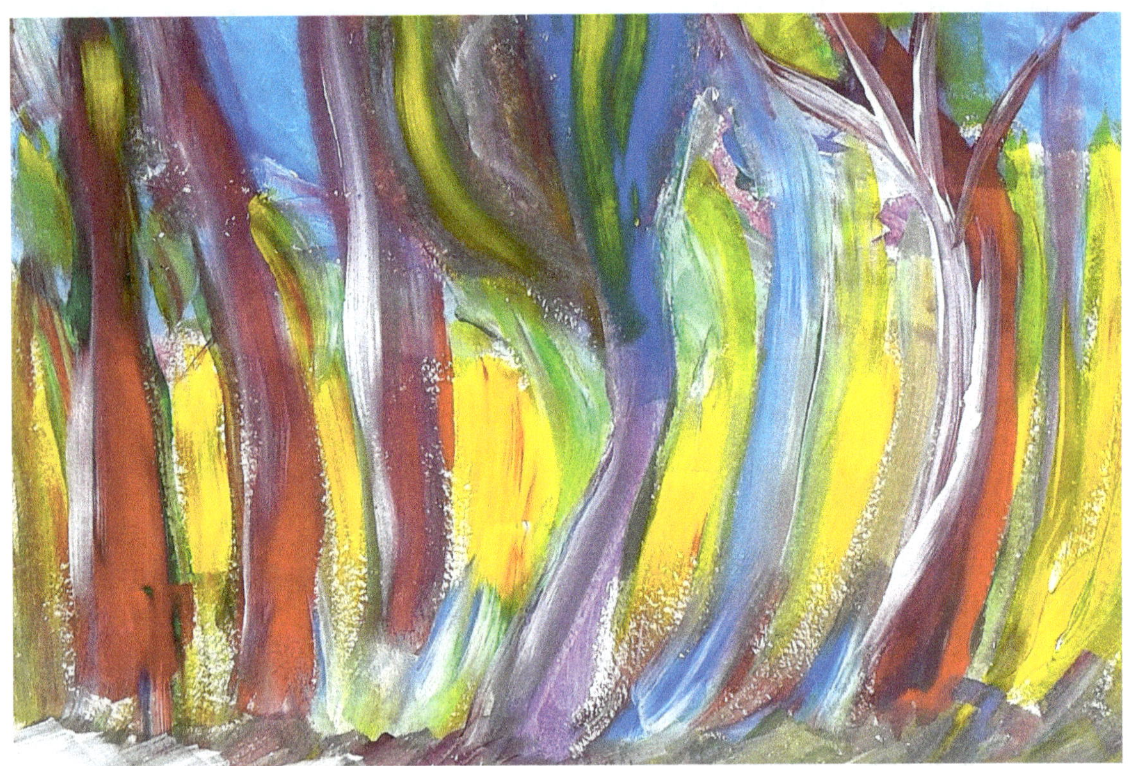

"Ribbons of Color"

White Feather

In a seagull's rush,
falling from the sky
through particles of dawn,
with no escape from gravity,
finally you come to rest on terra firma.

Blown here, blown there,
blown through the ventricles
of time's endless winding paths.

From close to heaven you came,
on whispers from God's breath.

Bending down and further still,
to see you closer,
I know you once kept a
winged creature warm.

But now you sit
upon the cold bare shore.

While nearby,
herons wade knee-deep,
fishing for their souls.

And I, alone . . .
a stranger cast adrift,
hold you tight . . .
for my salvation.

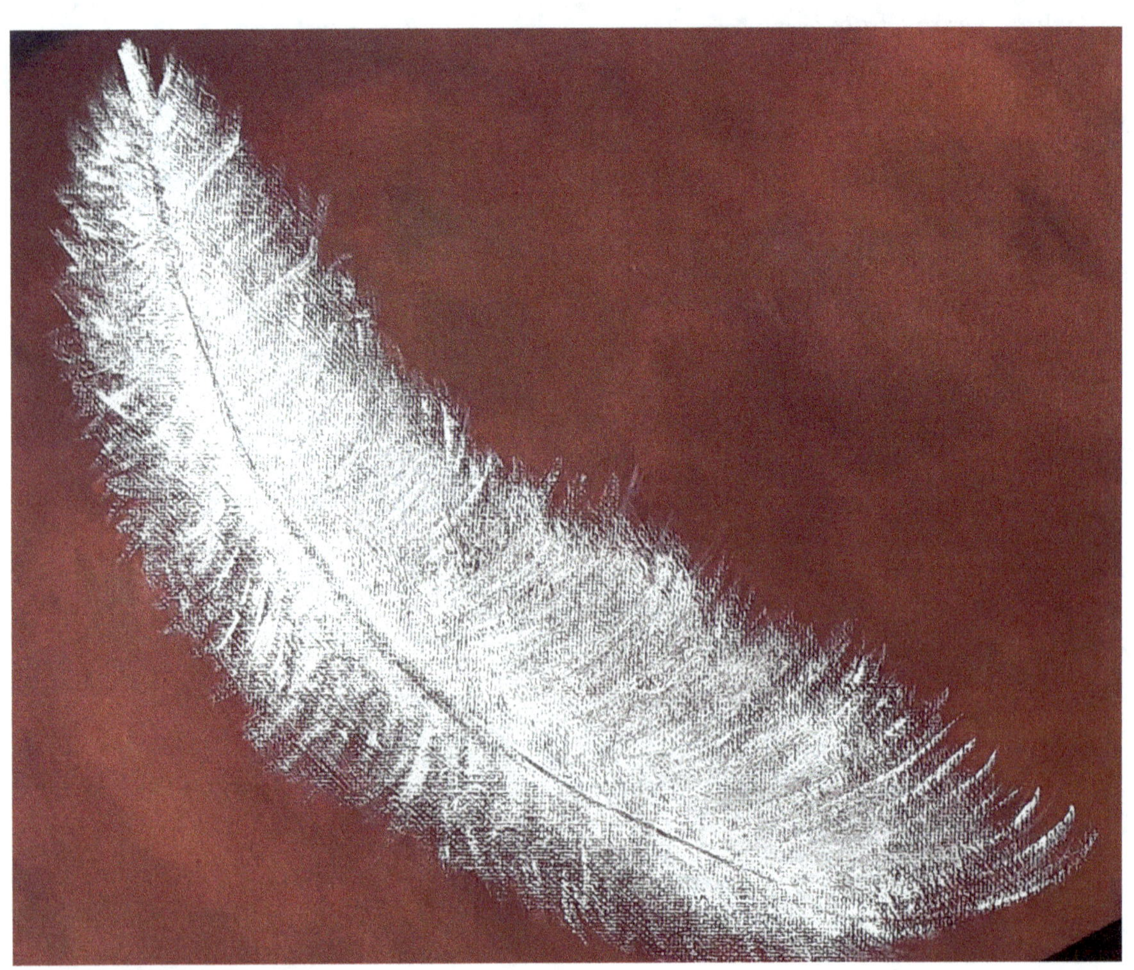

"White Feather"

Ode to Thomas Wolfe

He chose to look homeward.
An angel, his inspiration.
Asheville, his checkerboard.

Where there was a rhyme,
there was a reason.

The mind's a funny thing.
Once it grabs you, it's like a steel trap . . .
it never lets you go.

A perpetual rain of words poured forth,
like molasses, unstoppable.

In the end, his pen
was unforgiving.

No rest for the weary
until the final sleep.

And when it came, what he had done
left its mark on the sands of time.

A trumpet plays now somewhere,
probably in heaven.

For though his time was measured,
his soul was not.

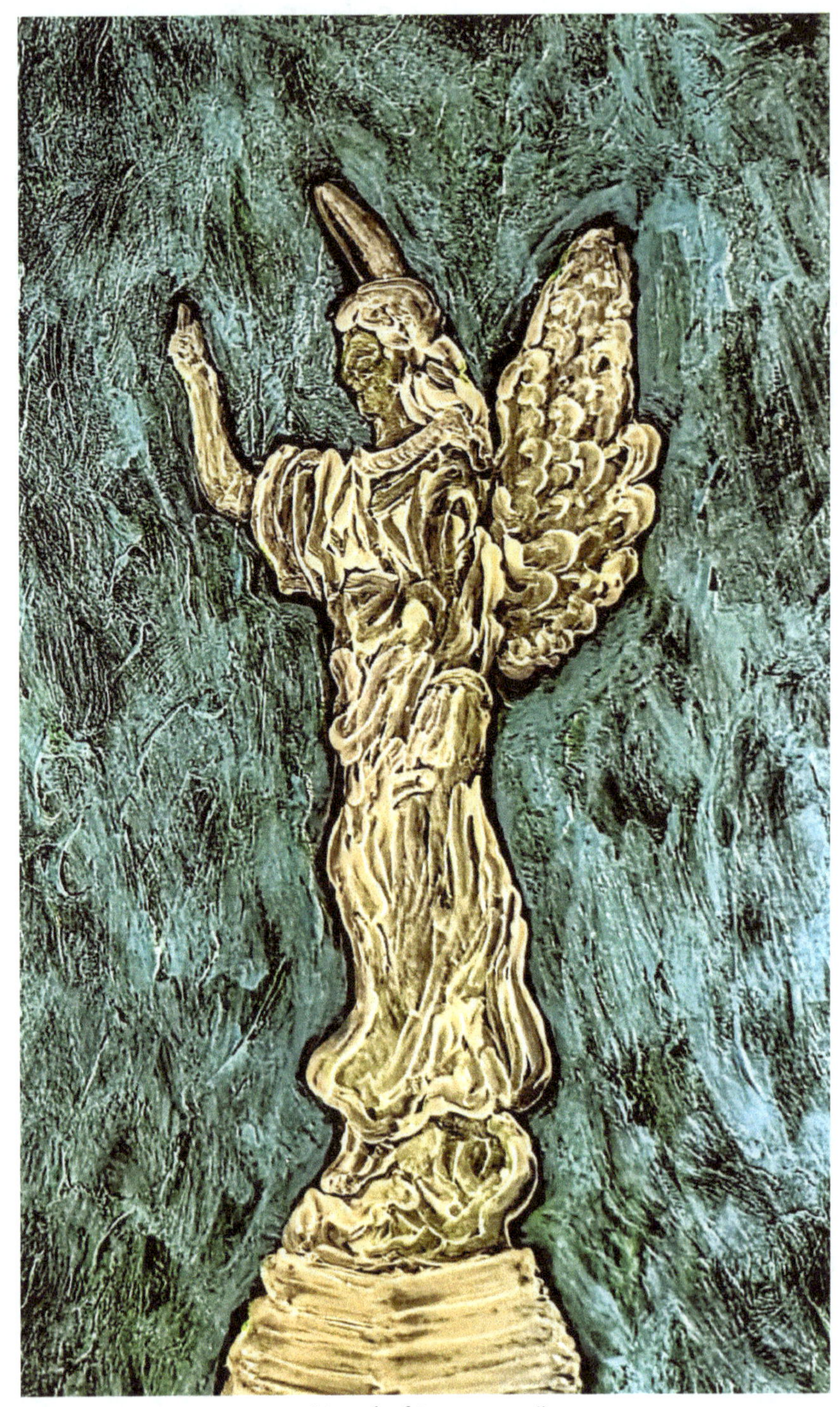

"Angel of Inspiration"

A Chimney Alone

A chimney stands alone in a field.
There had to have been a house. A home.
Where did it go?
"Do you know?" I ask the mountains.
Maybe it got washed away or came down in a flood long ago?

Stone upon stone. Climbing, all in a row.
Moss here, a vine there. That's all that's left now.
I ask the fields, "Do you know?"
They just continue to grow.

A chimney stands alone in a field weathering the ice and snow.
Another year has come. Spring has sprung.
I ask the trees, "Do you know?"
Firmly rooted to the earth. Some green, others bare.
Forlorn, they stare.

It must have seen the stars, felt the moon's glow.
"Do you know?" I ask the sky. "Where did it go?"
There must have been a house. A home, long ago.
But all that remains now is a chimney in a field.

These stones must have held a fireplace.
But now, in a field, you stand alone.
No walls. No windows, doors, or stove.
No floor. No home at all.

There had to have been calls from those next door.
Dreams and whispers across the floor.
Of another time.

Perhaps a family lived within these walls,
when life was simpler and horses rode the road,
and children learned their ABC's sitting on a stone.

People would come by to visit and say hello.
Yet somehow, you're all that remains.

When everything else is gone.
You are the last witness. To another time.
Another yesterday.

Now there's no fire burning in the stove.
You're all that's left.

A chimney alone.

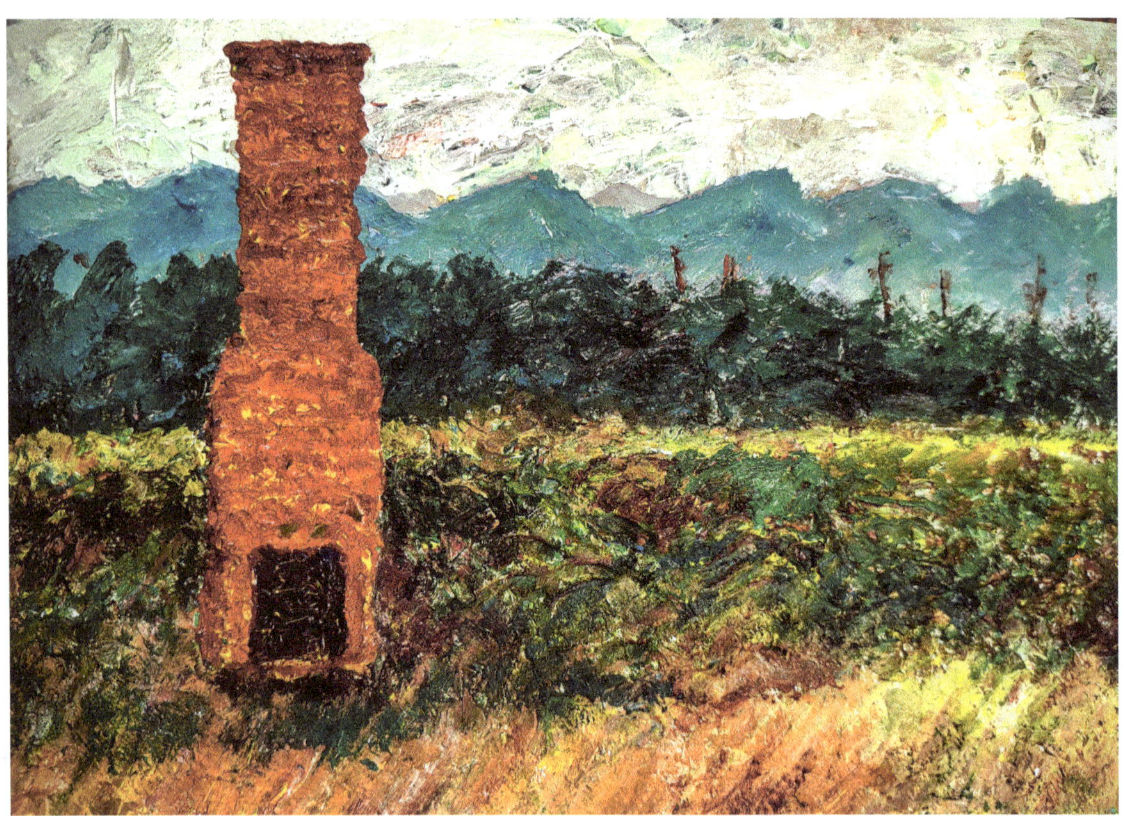

"A Chimney Alone"

Miracles Abound

Trees surround my vision singing in the morning's air,
molecules float effortlessly . . .
and I breathe again and again.

Nature plays one note after another on my soul
like Chopin; caressing, calming, capturing the light
of the new day's peace.

While my pen scratches on, swiftly meandering
into shapes of letters, expressions, capturing
what I feel inside.

The gift is the moment.
It's all we have.

In all its splendidness—giving without asking
anything in return.

While outside my window the trees arch towards the sky.
Branches curving upwards without movement.

Once a sapling, now a mighty oak, its surroundingly,
grooved heavy bark ready to weather the winter's approach,
stands effortlessly rooted to the earth.

As we dip and bend in the curvature of time.

Is there a reason? Is there a rhyme?
Round and round we go, where we stop,
no one knows.
A chickadee lands on a branch . . .

and then takes wing!

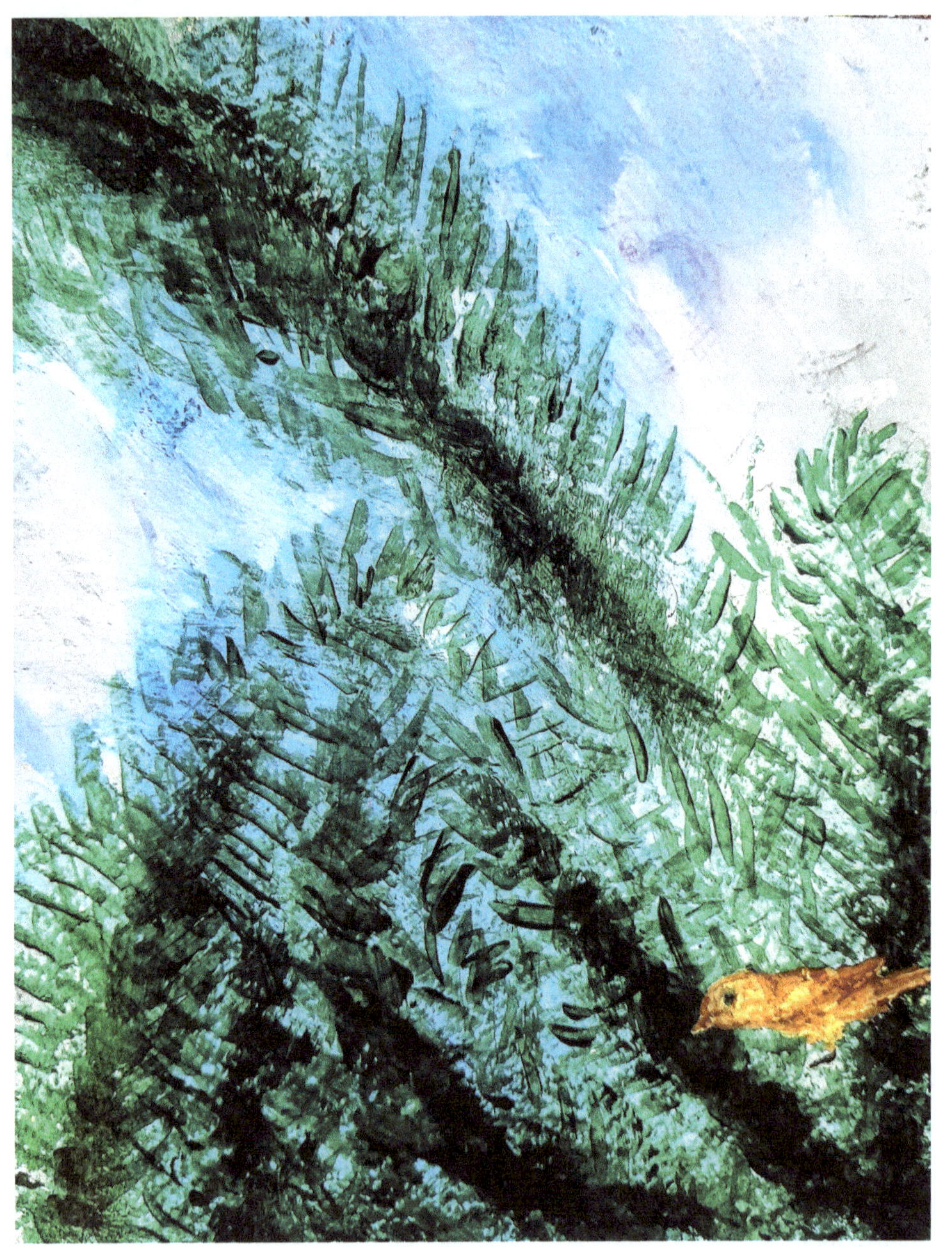

"A Chickadee Lands on a Branch"

Acknowledgments

"Ode to Edwin Booth" first appeared in "POEM", Huntsville Literary Association.

"As Angels Watched Overhead" was first published in "BEST POETS OF 2020", Eber & Wein Publishing.

"As I Step Out on Mostar Bridge" and the painting first appeared in "SOLO TRANSFORMATION ON STAGE", published by Sunbury Press.

"Ode to my Mother" was first published in "BEST POETS OF 2024", Eber & Wein Publishing.

All paintings and photographs by Ronald Rand, whose artist' name is Ronjay, are published with the permission of the artist.

"The Luthier" by Martha Carpenter. Courtesy of Martha Carpenter.

"Born to Fiddle" is a tribute to Donny Carpenter, fiddler of "Three Wheel Drive".

"Dancing Man" by Jean-Claude van Itallie. Courtesy of Jean-Claude van Itallie.

The Marsh in May & 30 Poems with 29 Paintings by Ronald Rand could only have been published with the faith of Dr. Lawrence Knorr, the Publisher of Sunbury Press, who believed in this book. I am honored and immensely grateful for his beautiful Foreword.

I am deeply indebted to my extraordinary editor, Olivia Neri, for her deep insight and thoroughness, my amazing graphic designer, Crystal Devine, Nicole Browne, John Jordan; and all those at Sunbury Press who have helped make *The Marsh in May & 30 Poems with 29 Paintings by Ronald Rand* as fine as it is.

I hold deep gratitude and love for those who have believed in my dreams—master artist and my mother, Maribee, and talented Janice—and all my friends and new friends who continue to inspire me every day with their kindness, love, and beauty.

Each day is filled with miracles, and I draw greater inspiration from nature for a deeper mindfulness to flow through me. Making me more aware of the earth's vibrations. Allowing my heart and soul to listen more deeply. Finding a deeper faith in the goodness of all those I meet. Believing in the kindness of all who live on this planet. We are all one.

About the Author

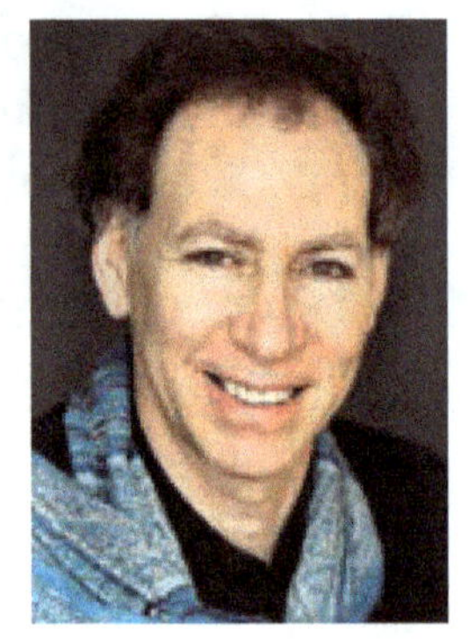

Ronald Rand is a US Cultural Ambassador and award-winning Solo Performing Artist. His poetry has been published in different poetry collections and his plays are performed around the world. While at NYU's Tisch School of the Arts, he studied at the Arts Student League in New York City with John Groth and several other teachers. His artwork has been exhibited in New York City, and across the country in museums, libraries and special exhibitions. The State Department and US Fulbright Program awarded him four Fulbright Awards as a Fulbright Specialist Scholar/Visiting Guest Professor in Malaysia, Uruguay, Greece, and Bosnia & Herzegovina. He currently tours around the world for over 25 years in his internationally acclaimed solo play, *LET IT BE ART!* bringing to life Harold Clurman, the "Elder Statesman of the American Theatre" in three critically acclaimed Off-Broadway productions, thirty countries, over twenty U.S. states, at more than a hundred theaters, universities, colleges and international festivals, and five tours across India. He was awarded the Jury Best Actor Award at the Bitola International Monodrama Festival in Macedonia. Founder & Publisher of "The Soul of the American Actor," Ronald is the author of *Solo Transformation on Stage*, *Acting Teachers of America*, *CREATE!*, and *The Marsh in May and 30 Poems with 29 paintings by Ronald Rand.* He is the Librettist of *IBSEN*, the first opera written about Henrik Ibsen, and the screenwriter of *GROUP PARADISE*, the first film about the famed Group Theatre of the 1930s. He has appeared in several Off-Broadway plays and regional productions, and in over a hundred films and TV shows including opposite Sean Connery and Dustin Hoffman in *Family Business*, Angelica Huston in *When in Rome*, Tom Cruise in *Vanilla Sky*, Yoko Ono in *Homeless*, Christopher Plummer in *O'Keefe & Stieglitz*, and Ralph Fiennes and Paul Scofield in *Quiz Show* directed by Robert Redford. An internationally acclaimed Stage Director, Master Acting Teacher, and Visiting Guest Professor at more than fifty universities and colleges, he has taught his "Art of Transformation" Workshop in 30 countries on five continents, including at The 30th anniversary LEAF Festival. LetItBeArt.com SoulAmericanActor.com IBSENopera.com CreatetheBook.com

www.ingramcontent.com/pod-product-compliance
Lightning Source LLC
LaVergne TN
LVHW080248110826
845148LV00023BA/868

* 9 7 9 8 8 8 8 1 9 3 2 3 5 *